Evangelism Explosion in Latin America

A creative concept to reach the world

Dr. Cecilio "Woody" N. Lajara

First edition, 2019

Spanish Paperback Version: ISBN 978-9929-647-15-2
English Paperback Version: ISBN 978-0-9988215-7-3

Dedicated

To my dear wife Carmen, my children Iris, Mariselle and John, who, when I went out to preach, to teach, to train pastors and leaders and evangelize, they stayed at home praying for me.

To my beloved disciples and pastors in Latin America, the Iberian Peninsula and the Hispanic Churches in the United States

Cover Cartoon

We express our gratitude to brother Luis Domingo Ordóñez (Mingo) for the cartoon he made during one of the first clinics in Buenos Aires, Argentina.

Index

Prologue

The story of the development of Evangelism Explosion throughout the world is very inspiring. It is full of experiences where men and women have put their lives on the line in every country on the Latin-American continent, Spain and Portugal. They have been arrested and charged by the police. Many times they had to sleep in uncomfortable places and with minimal facilities and sometimes the travel was unending.

God said "go" and a group of men and women were committed to the mandate of our Lord to equip his church to bring the Gospel to the "ends of the earth". In the E.E. office on McNab Street in Fort Lauderdale, Florida, the presence of the Lord was felt; one could feel the commitment of each member of the ministry to the Lord's mandate. It was in this environment that the Ministry of E.E. Latin America was born, equipping the churches to train their members to share the gospel of our Lord in places like the communist island of Cuba, or in Spain with very strong Catholicism and even in hedonistic places like Cancun, Mexico. These places became centers of E.E. development on the continent of Latin America.

When we write about the reality of a "dream" of continental expansion in Spain and Portugal, of a tool to prepare and train individuals to share the gospel of our Lord Jesus Christ, it cannot be communicated correctly without the participation of the one who dreams, who takes the vision to reality.

Although all praise and all the glory goes to Jesus Christ, who loves all people, not only in Latin America but around the world, we would be negligent if in the story of E.E. Latin America we did not include

Dr. Cecilio N. Lajara. The vision was marked in the heart of "Woody" the dreamer who led the expansion of E.E. to all corners of the world where Spanish and Portuguese are spoken.

In 1980, while attending an E.E. clinic in Coral Ridge Presbyterian Church in Fort Lauderdale, Florida, I asked the teachers if E.E. had plans to start E.E. in Latin America. I was told yes, but that it was necessary to get the person to lead this work in Latin America. I remember having said at that time: "If you find that person, please let him know that I will do everything I can to help him."

A few months after I returned to California, I received a phone call from a person whom I did not know. The person identified himself as "Woody" Lajara, who wished to visit me in California. He told me that he had recently been appointed as Vice President of E.E. for Latin America. He wanted to come to Fresno and discuss with me his plans for the development of E.E. in Latin America, Spain and Portugal.

When Woody came to my house, I noticed that he was more than just an executive with E.E. He was a person with passion, who loved the Lord and had a real vision for the development of E.E. in Latin America, which he shared faithfully with interested persons. On one occasion, while I walked down the hallway of the house and passed in front of the door of the room where Woody was, I saw that the door was closed. I stopped for a few moments and heard Woody talking. I realized that he was praying and talking with the Lord. The tone of his voice let me clearly see that he was praying for the leaders in Latin America with whom he was to communicate. He was weeping while mentioning names of leaders in the continent, Spain and Portugal. By then I understood that this brother who represented E.E. was more than a mere employee. He was a person who knew well and shared the vision and purpose for which Evangelism Explosion was established by its founder, Dr. D. J. Kennedy.

The first E.E. clinic in Spanish was held in Puerto Rico. Then they began to have clinics on the continent.

Woody faced several difficulties when they began ministry in some countries. For example, at the beginning of the first clinic in Ecuador, a church in Quito had volunteered to carry out the first clinic. As was the case in all clinics, materials were sent months in advance for the preparation of the local church that served as a "clinic base." The day before starting the clinic a meeting is held with the "Clinic Committee" to make all the preparations for the first day. When Woody requested that the CLINIC MANUAL be brought, the director said: "What manual?" Woody realized that the committee had not done the set-up work. So, Woody had to postpone the clinic for a day in which all the preparation was done. It was hard work, to review the Clinic Manual in one day when it was assumed that the Clinic Committee would study it months before. But God brought blessing in spite of everything.

When Woody came to Nicaragua (the country being under the regime of the Sandinistas) to introduce the ministry, an immigration officer at the airport put him under "house arrest" at the hotel where brother Lajara was going to stay. The officer assigned him a guard to prevent Dr. Lajara from visiting any pastor. The opportunity came when Woody made the presentation of the gospel to the guard, who accepted the gift of eternal life. Then the police asked for the list of pastors whom he called one by one asking them to come to the hotel for an interview. When in a communist country a person is called and asked to come for an interview it is something that must be obeyed exactly as requested. Thus Dr. Lajara spoke to the pastors presenting the ministry of E.E. Later the ministry of E.E. was begun in many churches in Nicaragua.

In Spain, as in many other countries, some pastors had developed a negative attitude towards E.E. which prevented E.E. from being introduced among them. But God had put in Woody's heart an idea that worked wonderfully among the pastors and leaders in Spain. After presenting a theological conference on how to fulfill the Great Commission, Woody invited several leaders to go out to make the presentation of the gospel. Some pastors accepted and went to practice. With great enthusiasm, they saw how several people accepted the "gift of eternal life." They saw how E.E. worked in their country. Then their interest grew in such a way that several clinics could be carried out, and many churches still continue to use E.E. to fulfill the Great Commission.

The story of the development of the Hispanic ministry of Evangelism Explosion in the United States, Latin America, Spain and

Portugal continues developing and growing. But instead of just reading what God has done through Woody and his team of workers, it would be much better for each of you to get involved in the ministry of the Great Commission using E.E. and let the world see that Christ lives and exists because He lives and exists in us.

Pastor Ray Castro
People's Church en Fresno, California

A manner of introduction

"But this is the covenant I will make with the people of Israel after those days ...." said Jehovah. *"I will put my law in their mind, and write it in their hearts; and I will be their God, and they will be my people."* (Jeremiah 31:33).

Evangelism Explosion International is a ministry that began in 1960 under the direction and leadership of Dr. D. James Kennedy, senior pastor of the Coral Ridge Presbyterian Church in Fort Lauderdale, Florida.

One Sunday night, Dr. Kennedy, before a faithful group of about 15 people gathered in one of the classrooms of one of the schools in Fort Lauderdale, Florida, read from the Old Testament God's promises to the prophet: *"Call to me, and I will answer you, and **tell you great** and unsearchable **things** that you do not know"* (Jeremiah 33:3). Then Dr. Kennedy closed the Bible and looking at the faithful group who were there he said: "Do you know something? I think we can change the world!"

In 2004, an incredulous reporter (in the form of sarcasm) told Dr. Kennedy, "It seems that you are trying to Christianize America." Dr. Kennedy responded with a smile: "No sir, I'm not trying to change America, I'm trying to change the world."

The vision of the ministry of Evangelism Explosion manifests the vision of being able to change the world. The vision is manifested in this way: "Every nation, equipping all the ethnic groups, of all ages, to testify to everyone."

Our goal is to see everyone on earth facing the opportunity to receive the good news of the Gospel of our Lord Jesus Christ. We also believe that the church is the vehicle that God will use for this to happen. Therefore, our vision is to be active participants, to change the world as a promoter of the church of Christ, seeking to become a multiplier church to help others do the same.

Since its inception, the ministry has literally grown to cover the world. By 1996 it had already reached all the nations of the world, becoming the first ministry that has reached the whole world being active in all the nations of the world. During our 55-year history, for the glory of God, we have trained millions of Christians to be witnesses for Christ throughout the world.

The ministry of E.E. in Latin America officially began in 1980 when Dr. Cecilio (Woody) Lajara came to be the Vice President for Latin America. His first task was to finish the translation that an Impact missionary had begun, but Dr. Lajara had to start practically from the beginning, together with a group of brothers who were interested in the task.

By 1983 E.E. had been planted in every country of the continent. The initial response to E.E. from pastors and leaders of the continent was very positive. Even several evangelical denominations decided to take E.E. as a tool to train their respective leaders in evangelization.

Why has Evangelism Explosion been able to develop well in the continent? Naturally there are several reasons, but certainly the leadership has been a very strong and markedly successful factor, starting with the first Vice President, Dr. Cecilio (Woody) Lajara. As he frequently said: "*My blood is E.E. positive!*"

Woody helped train and prepare the second E.E. Vice President for Latin America, Will Rodriguez. Will also shares Woody's passion for evangelization and rejoices when people accept the gift of eternal life. Through these and many other leaders in the continent the ministry continues its development for the glory of God. As is our vision for other parts of the world, we want to see many people across Latin America come to the feet of the Lord. GLORY TO GOD!

Dr. John B. Sorensen
president@eeworks.org
President of Evangelism Explosion International

EE Hispanic work team

This book has a simple purpose: to reveal what was done during the development of the ministry of Evangelism Explosion on the continent of Latin America, Hispanic USA and the Iberian Peninsula. What motivated the production of this book has been the request of several brothers who wanted to have in their hands the story of this impacting ministry.

Several members of the E.E. work team have participated in this book as well as other leaders involved since the beginning of the ministry. Some of them have written part of the story of the ministry to which God has called us to serve our continent and the Iberian Peninsula. To these leaders I am most grateful for the work done to achieve our purpose. Thank you.

These people are:

Dr. Pablo Méndez Nieto y su esposa Argelia	Columbia
Rev. Roberto Searing	Columbia
Dr. Juan Calcagni	Argentina
Dr. Guillermo DiGiovanna	Southern Cone
Rev. David Gómez	Ethnic Director
Ing. Nahúm Vega y su esposa Cristina	Mexico
Rev. Valentin Vale	Venezuela
Dr. Ernesto Humeniuk	Argentina
Pastor Juan Diego Vallejos	Iberian Peninsula
Rev. Ray Castro	USA Hispano
Miss Minette Malaret	Administrative Assistant

Other members of the E.E. Latin America Work Team have been: Dr. Osvaldo Casati (ya con el Southern Cone Señor)

Rev. Edwin Gant	First Hispanic USA Director
Sr. Libardo Barrios	Second Director of Columbia
Rev. Guillermo Hernández	First Director for Central America
Rev. Rolando Alvarez	Second Director for Central America

Biographical summary fo Dr. D. James Kennedy (1930-2007)

First, I want to introduce brother James (Jim) Kennedy and how God used him to begin the ministry of Evangelism Explosion.

James Kennedy grew up in Chicago in his childhood and in Tampa, Florida in his youth, where he attended the University of Tampa, with a scholarship in music. At that time music bands were well known and many people learned to dance in the "Arthur Murray" studio where Jim Kennedy was one of the best dance instructors. He mastered all the dance steps and became a renowned national dance competitor and instructor in the studios of "Arthur Murray."

One night a young lady, Anne Lewis, entered the studio in Tampa to receive lessons from the young instructor. Jim Kennedy, then 22 years old, told a friend when he saw her enter, "that's the girl who I'm going to marry." During their first conversation, Anne, who was a Christian, confronted young Kennedy about what he believed and based his way of life. Although he believed in God and assumed he was a Christian, Anne's question made him think. At that time Jim had not yet accepted Jesus Christ as his Savior.

One Sunday afternoon, after waking with a severe headache (because of having too much to drink the day before), Jim began to listen to a radio program hosted by Dr. Donald Gray Barnhouse, pastor of the 10th Presbyterian Church of Philadelphia. Dr. Barnhouse asked the following question: *"Imagine that you were to die today and you appeared before God, who asked you: 'Why should I let you into my kingdom?'*

What would you say?"

The young Kennedy heard Barnhouse's explanation about salvation and redemption. Sitting on the edge of his bed and paying close attention, he listened to Dr. Barnhouse. He thought, "I never thought of things like these. I searched for answers, but nothing ever happened". Thinking that he did not have the right to "enter heaven" he gave his life to Christ, accepting him as Savior.

His life changed that moment, as if it were a miracle. The change was 180 degrees, said Dr. Kennedy, who had friends who didn't know what had happened to him. One moment there was a young man leading an "Arthur Murray" Dance Center interested in things of this world and suddenly there is a change in his life. A new creature was born and the old creature died. James Kennedy said he had become a "new creature".

Soon after this change, he went to visit Anne with an engagement ring in hand and he said: "I have quit my job at the Arthur Murray Studio, which means I have no income. But I am going to enter the ministry and I know that you always said you wanted to be a pastor's wife. Will you marry me?" Of course, Anne was surprised but said yes.

James Kennedy went to study at Columbia Theological Seminary in Decatur, Georgia, receiving his Master of Divinity. It was the same seminar where I was blessed to study several years later.

After graduating from Seminary, they went to the city of Fort Lauderdale, Florida to begin the "Coral Ridge" Presbyterian Church. The attendance in the first meeting was about 45 people. After ten months of hard work, the attendance dropped to 17 participants. Dr. Kennedy and his wife were frustrated.

Then Dr. Kennedy went to the city of Atlanta to conduct an evangelistic campaign with his friend Dr. Kennedy Smartt who he observed carefully in his work. The two went out during the day to visit many people in their homes. Then he understood and recognized that what was needed for evangelization was to win people "one by one".

Upon his return to Fort Lauderdale he reviewed what he learned in Atlanta with Rev. Kennedy Smartt and formulated the method of Evangelism Explosion. Then he began to teach the leaders of his congregation to win people one by one. In one month his church grew from 17 to 66 people; then it grew to 122 the following year. When they reached 200 members, they gave themselves the task of organizing the "Coral Ridge Church," which became the fastest growing church in South Florida. By 1974 they had a church of 3,000 members.

Pastors and leaders from everywhere wanted to know how this growth came about. Then Dr. Kennedy began the ministry of conducting "clinics " to train leaders from everywhere. The first of these clinics took place in the month of February 1967. In this first clinic there was an attendance of 36 pastors and leaders. Since then they have trained hundreds of thousands of pastors and leaders worldwide in clinics led by Evangelism Explosion International.

Dr. Kennedy invited me in 1972 to participate with him

When I was participating as representative in one of the first General Assemblies of our denomination, Presbyterian Church of America (PCA), I met Dr. D. James Kennedy and he told me he wanted to talk with me. We agreed on the day and time, and there we had the first meeting where I learned the first details of the ministry of **Evangelism Explosion**; it was my first contact with the ministry of Evangelism Explosion. This was in 1972 in the city of Birmingham, Alabama.

Dr. Kennedy, in a very kind way, explained the projections of Evangelism Explosion International, extending me an invitation to participate in the next E.E. clinic in Coral Ridge Church during the month of August 1972. There I received the first instructions of E.E. under the teachings of Dr. Kennedy and Dr. Archie Parrish, who was then the International Director of E.E.

The experience was very good and I was able to use what I learned during my first period of missionary work in Mexico, as professor of theology at the Presbyterian Seminary in Mexico City. In my free time I helped pastors in several churches and there I could implement what I had learned with Dr. Kennedy and Dr. Parrish.

Then, in 1976, our Mission Board of P.C.A., M.T.W. agreed to send us to Guatemala, where God gave me the opportunity to establish the School of Theology at the Mariano Gálvez University.

In 1979, when I was doing missionary work in the United States, raising funds for our missionary support, Dr. Kennedy and Dr. Archie Parrish extended me an invitation to translate the materials of E.E. and begin the ministry of E. E. in Latin America. It was a very interesting challenge, because the ministry of E.E. was practically in its beginnings.

I met a missionary who worked with Bruce Woodman (Del Monte)'s Impact Ministry, brother Estrie Britton, who had already begun the translation of the textbook, Evangelism Explosion, but did not make much progress. I took the responsibility of translation and the direction of the ministry.

There was an agreement of our Mission Board (M.T.W.) with Evangelism Explosion so that I could begin my next full-time missionary work with Evangelism Explosion International. My family and I moved to Fort Lauderdale, Florida and began working with E. E. in August 1980. I came to be part of the International Task Team of Evangelism Explosion under the direction of Dr. Archie Parrish. My responsibilities had to do with the Vice Presidency of Evangelism Explosion for Latin America, in addition to sharing other responsibilities with Dr. James Kennedy's team.

I always heard Dr. Kennedy say that evangelization was the task of the laity, and the ministry of E.E. was created specifically to train the laity to do the work of evangelization.

Dr. Billy Graham, referring to Dr. Kennedy, puts it this way: "No one has seen this more clearly, nor has he used it more successfully than Dr. James Kennedy, Presbyterian pastor, who in nine years has seen his congregation grow from a simple mission almost without members to a church of two thousand members." According to Dr. Graham, "Dr. Kennedy has recaptured the biblical concept that the primary task of the church is that each member evangelizes." [1]

On the other hand, Dr. Kennedy writes: "In the middle of 1969, at the **World Consultation of Evangelism** held in Switzerland, it was emphasized that the 60s was characterized by the emergence of the work of the laity in the church, because of their interest in evangelism. Around 1960, a number of different groups and movements in various parts of the world came up with the same vision: the mobilization and training of a vast army of lay people to the task of ministry."[2]

---

[1] Billy Graham, El Mundo en Llamas [*World Aflame*], (Buenos Aires, Sopena editorial, Argentina, 1967), p. 15

[2] D. James Kennedy, Evangelism Explosion, (Wheaton, Tyndale House Publishers, 1970) p, 1

By the end of the 1950s and then in the following decades, the growth and notoriety of evangelization in the continent of Latin America was very marked. We need to consider and point out the beginnings of evangelistic associations and groups born in the heat of the blaze by the evangelization, producing in turn a strong interest and growth overall in the great commission.

The historical context of those years

Let's take a quick look at the historical context that served as the cradle for the beginning of the ministry of Evangelism Explosion in our Latin America, or as I usually call it, "Brown America" (América Morena).

I remember that by the time we started the ministry of Evangelism Explosion in Latin America, we were generally experiencing moments of great interest about the fulfillment of the Great Commission. They were times when there was a boom for the **"evangelistic campaigns"**. Evangelists such as Luis Palau, the Mottesi brothers, the Billy Graham team, Fernando Vangioni from Argentina, Daniel Altares and Samuel Libert, also from Argentina, and others, were very busy conducting great evangelistic campaigns in various parts of our land in Latin America.

It is worth mentioning that on the "Isle of Enchantment", Puerto Rico, there was a great evangelistic advance with brother Rev. Yiye Avila. Generally, their campaigns throughout the Latin American continent were carried out with the pentecostal or pentecostal revival churches. I remember when I was living in Guatemala I had the opportunity to attend a Yiye Avila campaign programmed by the pentecostal churches.

In 1946, Dr. Billy Graham, beginning his evangelistic ministry under the direction of **"*YOUTH FOR CHRIST*"** began the formation of a work team composed of him, Cliff Barrows and George Beverly Shea. They began to carry out "evangelistic campaigns" of one week, some of two and three weeks in several cities in the United States. The evangelistic crusade in the city of Los Angeles, California was a great experience for Dr. Graham. By the end of the third week, total attendance had passed 100,000 people with more than 1,500 decisions. The **Billy Graham Evangelistic Association** was organized in 1951. They have had the blessing of conducting evangelistic campaigns on all continents of the world. It has been a blessing for evangelistic advancement.

One of the organizations that has greatly helped evangelistic work in our beautiful "Brown America" has been what we have known as *"EVANGELISM IN DEPTH"* (EVAF, Evangelismo a Fondo). God blessed this evangelistic effort as a contribution of evangelization means of our Latin America to the world, since *EVAF* reached worldwide movements.

The founder of EVAF, Kenneth Strachan, dreamed of the plan to engage and use all the evangelical forces of a country. His ambitious goal was to mobilize a nation to fulfill the evangelizing task. Evangelism in Depth was spread throughout the continent covering several Latin American countries.

His primary emphasis was known as *"The Strachan Theorem: the growth of any movement is in direct proportion to the success it has in mobilizing its members in the constant propagation of its beliefs..."* God has used Evangelism in Depth in such a way that it has become a worldwide movement and we give glory to God for the development of this ministry.

Another movement that arises about this same time was created by our Lord through brother Bill Bright, known as **"CAMPUS CRUSADE FOR CHRIST"**.

It was born at the University of California primarily as a movement to evangelize students at the University. Dr. Bright and his wife began this ministry in a rented house near the University and there they gave themselves to the task of evangelization in 1951. In the first year they had more than 250 students who accepted Christ. There, in his limited beginnings, he began a Crusade that later spread throughout the world with very important results with more than 1,500 workers in hundreds of universities in the United States and in 40 countries.

On the other hand, we must mention the team of evangelist Luis Palau, who has had considerable success in his campaigns with the use of television for evangelization.

The evangelistic advance has become evident in the celebration of some national and international conferences on evangelism. I have had the blessing to participate in some of them.

In 1966 the first of such conferences was held in Berlin where more than 500 delegates, observers and journalists came from 104 countries; we were 133 church leaders of our "Brown" America. This was the first time that in modern times there was a meeting of this magnitude where leaders of various theological positions from different parts of the world participated. I still remember the words of one of the leaders and expositors, Dr. Harold J. Ockenga who declared:

"Evangelism is based on four convictions: men are lost; God loves them; the leap of faith in confession and repentance; and the life of obedience". [3]

I remember one of the emphasis during the Congress was on the presence of the Holy Spirit in the believer's life, extremely important for evangelization. My good friend and fellow militia, Dr. Fernando Vangioni, said: "May our lives be fully surrendered to the Holy Spirit, to demonstrate what we preach. Then the Holy Spirit accompanies the Word with its power ... only then will the world listen to what it needs: the voice of God and not of man ... "

We cannot ignore the United State Congress on Evangelism. It had an interdenominational character, which contributed greatly to the large growth of evangelism that began after this Congress. The Congress originated in the Lutheran Church in America, and was marked by the parameters of the Billy Graham Evangelistic Association. There were about five thousand delegates from all of the United States, plus leaders from other parts of the evangelical world.

One important point for me were the words of Dr. Leighton Ford who said at the end of his conference: "If our lives and our churches have ceased to fulfill the revolutionary expectations of God, what is the reason behind it? Is it not perhaps that we have not allowed the Holy Spirit to control us, the directing agent of God's strategy?"[4]

During this period there were other regional conferences on evangelism. Unfortunately, I was not able to attend all of them, although I would have liked to be present. One I could not leave aside

[3] Harold J. Okenga, paper presented at the World Evangelization Congress, Berlin, October, 1966.

[4] Leighton Ford, "Evangelism in a Day of Revolution," paper presented at the American Congress of Evangelism, Sep. 1969.)

was CLADE, "Congreso Latinoamericano de Evangelismo" (Latin American Congress of Evangelism) held in Bogotá, Colombia November 21-30 1969.

We were about a thousand delegates and visitors, representing almost all the Latin American denominations and evangelical groups as well as Spanish-speaking leaders in the United States.

We gathered there in Colombia to study and review our ministry under the theme: "Action in Christ for a Continent in Crisis". The congress was organized under the leadership of the Billy Graham Association and the Latin American Mission in San José, Costa Rica. A Puerto Rican friend, who extended me a special invitation, was Dr. Carlos Lastra, who was the Vice President of the Congress. The supremacy of the Holy Spirit was generally emphasized in the evangelizing action, and unity was very marked among groups of diverse theological positions. This event was, without a doubt, a historic and decisive congress in the development of the movement in our countries and, of course, contributed greatly to the willingness of the churches on our continent, to open their doors for a training program such as Evangelism Explosion.

I have tried to document somewhat the time when we started and developed Evangelism Explosion. We lived moments when we sought an "explosion of evangelism" in almost every church and denomination on the continent. At those times we almost forgot our theological differences and we offered our hand to work together.

I remember that the meeting in Berlin (where I believe the movement began) was where we saw it with our own eyes. Then this emphasis was manifested in Minneapolis and later in **C.L.A.D.E. in Colombia**. Not that we put aside our theological convictions, which define our thinking and our walk with Christ, but we have allowed the manifestation of the Holy Spirit in us, who joined us together as the true Body of Christ.

This unity was very significant if we remember that it was very difficult for the brothers of the "Reformed" tradition to gather with the "Pentecostal" brothers to work together. But for the time of the birth of Evangelism Explosion, there was a consensus of unity.

I remember in Puerto Rico, in the first clinic in the First Baptist

Church of Rio Piedras, a couple of Pentecostal brothers, as they washed their hands in the bathroom, commented, "Hey, this Dr. Lajara ¿Is he Pentecostal?" The other replied: "I don't know. I think he is Presbyterian...but he must be a revived Presbyterian."

Always my teachings, and in the development of the ministry, we manifested Christ as Lord and Savior of all. Our emphasis was always to honor Christ, to fulfill His mandate of the Great Commission, to present a Christ who died for all, for His Church which he has called and chosen to continue working in the ministry that He began in the establishment of His Kingdom. Yes, our emphasis was well marked in presenting our Savior, but the Savior of all sinners. This commission was given to the whole church, not just a chosen group.

Therefore, all of us, Presbyterians, Pentecostals, Armenians, Reformed, in short, we all have the responsibility of fulfilling the Great Commission and it is extremely important that we train all the brothers to carry out this important task.

There are some leaders who thought they had achieved what God required of them about the Great Commission at those moments of great evangelistic breakthrough in the 1960s and 1970s. They believed that the movement of evangelization had reached such intensity and had obtained so many good results, but many went to sleep contemplating their accomplishments and thanking God.

But in Evangelism Explosion we believe the opposite. It was necessary to continue equipping the brothers in the local churches to continue fulfilling the Great Commission. This is ongoing work until the Second Coming of the Lord. It was true that we then lived positive moments with great blessing, but we could only see that the church experienced a certain "revival" in view of its responsibility and evangelistic potential and that many were blessed by it.

An old friend, Dr. Emilio Núñez (of Guatemala) said: "This is not new, but once again we had the experience of personal involvement, the training, and complete security of the presence of Christ in us, which leads us to the personal winning of souls. They aren't just additional activities in the congregations, but the very center of the entire life of the churches."

We give glory to God because our emphasis in Evangelism

Explosion was to train and equip the brothers of the churches to accomplish the task of evangelization as we were sent by the Lord.

Chapter 1

Our task in evangelism

We live in times of crisis, but it is not because of the nature of the desperate crisis in which we live that the task of evangelization, which the Lord commanded us, is urgent today. The urgency of evangelization, or evangelistic task of the Church, comes from the very Gospel, because it is the Gospel and the command of the Lord himself. Christ loves this world, for which he died to save it. He is the Light of the world of which He is the Lord. His light precedes the mandate of the good news facing the darkness of the world.

The Christian's task is to be a witness to his light, which shines by pointing to the path of salvation. In Christ there is life, which became the light of men, the light that guides all men. The task of evangelization is very important in this and all ages so that the blind can see and follow Christ in the establishment of the Kingdom of God.

However, the urgency in which we find ourselves has to pinpoint for Christians their responsibilities and opportunities to fulfill the task of evangelizing. This world has become, for the first time in history, a completely interdependent world, in which people of all latitudes must solve our problems among us if we do not want to perish without fulfilling our responsibilities in evangelization.

We live in moments of revolution, where important changes are emerging in all areas of human life. We, the Christians, know that God is the God of history therefore difficult times in our history do not go outside the limits of the protection of the Creator. Even these moments are under the control of our Lord. Therefore, moments of crisis become opportunities to testify and seek the direction of our Lord. We continue our lives guided by the Holy Spirit, who directs us to where Christ is and will help us to fulfill the evangelization. The darkness of this world cannot overcome the Light of Christ that shines through his people at all times.

Currently the task of evangelization has to be carried out in several places and using new strategies. The church in various locations recognizes that new challenges require new ways to fulfill evangelization, following new appropriate forms and understanding sympathy with all those involved in their aspirations and sufferings and with fresh determination to talk to people about the truth of the Gospel where they live. Evangelism Explosion may very well adapt in all areas of life or in all historical moments of humanity. Let us remember that the intervention of the Holy Spirit is present at all times when the presentation of the gospel is made. This is an extremely important factor in fulfilling the Great Commission.

The church knows that the outcome of its mission depends totally on God and not the wiles and adaptabilities in the effort to co-exist with other ideologies, whether scientific, technological, nationalist, political, or religious. The church knows that it can very faithfully testify of the true Light only in absolute obedience to the voice of the Living God. It also recognizes that, although evangelization strategies and techniques may change, the Gospel it proclaims does not change, for it is the unchanging Gospel of God's love to redeem the world through Christ, manifested to us through the Holy Spirit.

Jesus of Nazareth, the Christ, is the Universal Lord and Savior of the world. This is part of our common faith and we confirm it every time we carry out and celebrate the worship service every Sunday. We assert with all hope in his Second Coming that we have the blessing of being with Him. Therefore, it remains the interest of the Father that everyone know Jesus as Savior and the redemption of the world is accomplished.

We say these words about Christ, not about us. We are not the "Savior of the world." We are called to testify of Him as Savior and Lord of all. We cannot be his witnesses without being completely under his light and his direction.

The good news about Christ is relevant to everyone in all ages, therefore, it must be communicated in different ways adapted to different times and cultures. The Holy Spirit makes this possible in every age and in every culture. It is interesting that training each individual to reach their peers has been the way that adapts best, even in all periods of time, for the training of the faithful followers of Christ, in a personal way. This is why Evangelism Explosion was and has been so effective in training and equipping the brothers in the churches, in different cultures and even in different periods of time.

Communicating the gospel involves the willingness and ability of the followers of Christ to identify with sinners. Making a good identification with the person is something essential and important in communicating the gospel. Thus the evangelist has to reveal or communicate, that the message he presents is not his own message, but the real and authentic message of salvation of our Savior. It is as if one beggar told another beggar where to find the bread of life that meets his needs. It is important in this type of communication to look for a common language where the speaker can communicate without problems with his listeners. The true biblical message of salvation can be communicated in words and forms of the century in which we live. Evangelism Explosion has been adapted for use in various cultures and in different situations. Just as we cannot expect humanity to understand the biblical vocabulary it is very necessary to adapt our verbal expression to everyday vernacular.

The sharing of the gospel must be examined by the gospel itself. Communication involves more than merely talking. Our message should be part of our body movements, the confidence with which we speak, the expressive forms and gestures of truth that we use. The church, manifested in local congregations, may very well obscure or clarify the saving message of the Lord. The spectators will forget their own judgments according to what they see in these congregations. The worship service, unity and common life of congregations are very important factors in the evangelization of each church. Our message has not been truly proclaimed until the "listener" can live it in his own life. Naturally, we must be sure that it is Christ and not "Christianity" that we are proclaiming as the true message of the Lord. It is the power of God and not ours that has to bring people to Christ's feet.

Experiments have been carried out in various parts of the world using dialogue as a special means in the search for good communication. Some have been good and successful; others have not achieved what they set out to do. I do not intend to judge their values, but we do rejoice because they have given much encouragement and great help in the process of evangelizing. For us, dialogue in Evangelism Explosion presentation has been very effective in all parts of the world where we have implemented it.

It is impossible to speak of evangelization and Christian communication without mentioning radio, television, and the press. At first glance we thought it has little to do with personal dialogue, but if we look closer, we realize that in each there is some "dialogue" expressed that involves the "listening", the "reader" and the one who "watches television".

Although we are living in revolutionary times, as we have said, we are sure that God is very busy working on all the great changes that are taking part in our history. Christian communication has to be affected in the orbit of these changes. Times of revolution are precisely times when, if opportunities arise, God's purpose can be proclaimed to the world that will be shaken in its principles during the events of any day.

The mandate to evangelize is given to all members of the church. It is a commission given to the whole church to bring the gospel to all creatures throughout the world. When the church understands that it exists to accomplish this task, a passion and interest arises to bring the gospel to all countries and all creatures. These blessings, such as the alleviation of poverty, sickness, hunger, and the creation of true fellowship, can very well eliminate the loneliness and depression of the masses in our society. Christian evangelization becomes a privilege for mankind, supported by the immense love of our God. It is not us who take Christ to men, but it is Christ himself who uses us as agents of his work for them. The evangelizing work of the church is to provide the whole gospel to the world, not merely those easy to reach places, because the unity of the church is bound to the unity of the gospel. It cannot be divided or shared in expressions of scientific studies and social organizations. Its convergent points in the secular work can become great possibilities and opportunities for the evangelistic work of the church.

To be truly effective, the lay testimony must arise from the true understanding of the Gospel, in such a way that it can be clearly communicated and articulated in an understandable language and that the listeners recognize the importance of it. Only the laity can communicate with their peers and discuss matters in which they are involved. You can show that the message of the gospel of Jesus Christ is highly relevant to their current needs.

In the ministry of Evangelism Explosion, we have seen that the laity, who recognize their own responsibilities to fulfill the evangelization, welcome the training openly. Many of them have been very eager to clarify their minds, remove their perplexities about the Bible, theology, ethics, and others, and in a very frank and firm way be able to speak to others about the Savior.

The pastors, having a great desire to see their congregations grow, have been a great help providing guidance to these laity, although some have done it in an egocentric way, to see growth in their congregations. Naturally, others have sought to fulfill the Great Commission and have had a marked success in their efforts.

To mention some of them, let me mention pastor Samuel Olson of Las Acacias Church in Caracas, Venezuela. Brother Samuel, after attending an E.E. clinic in Fort Lauderdale, returned to his congregation with great expectations and the blessing of the Lord. He began with great enthusiasm motivating other leaders, especially the pastor of evangelism of the congregation, brother Santiago Montero. As a result, there was a marked growth of new people who accepted the gift of eternal life. They continued the training by having two training periods per year until they became a clinic base. The first E.E. clinic was organized in Las Acacias with an attendance of 82 participating leaders. I remember that they had to close the inscriptions on the date marked, although they continued to receive applications from people who wanted to participate in the clinic. Then they continued to have clinics every year until other clinic bases emerged there in Caracas as in other cities in Venezuela.

As I mentioned already, pastors can be a great help in the preparatory work for Evangelism Explosion training. It is important that the pastor provide a good example and interest in the fulfillment of the Great Commission, if he wishes to train lay people in his congregation and in the fulfillment of the Great Commission. Pastors and laity need to learn to work as a team, each recognizing the importance of the participation of the other, seeing and understanding that each has the responsibility of exercising the gifts that by grace have been provided by God in the expectation of being used by them for the growth of the Body of Christ.

There is an urgent need to recover the true meaning of certain biblical words: to recognize and understand that the laity are the true "Laos", I mean, the people of God present in the world, naturally including those who have been ordained, exercising their particular abilities and their gifts, helping their Christian brothers in the name of Christ. This can create fellowship and a good relationship between the brothers in the congregation. This is what happens in those congregations that begin E. E. with emphasis on the fulfillment of the Great Commission, which leads to such a congregation to become what we call a "clinic base".

If this penetration into the world by the laity of the churches is an essential part of the plan of God for their churches, it is very necessary to examine the conventional structures of our churches to see and understand if the churches are being a stumbling block or are helping to carry out the plan of God for evangelization. We cannot think that the churches are mere gothic or contemporary buildings, nor can we think of the churches as mere ecclesiastical structures led by theologians and administrators. We can easily think of the church as the group that meets every Sunday for a worship service, but this is not right. The church is composed of laymen who are scattered throughout society, attending their own daily jobs, provided by God, but are laymen who have a living relationship with the Lord as Savior. Often certain scandals may arise in the minds of believers that prevent a positive reaction to the manifestation of our Lord's saving message and impeding the possibilities of making a good presentation of the salvific message of our Lord.

It is very important that the church of Christ, always in obedience to the Lord, face the changes in society with confidence and certainty to be the key to provide the necessary stability in the world in which we live.

This revolutionary era confronts the church and all creation with great opportunities and challenges to serve and therefore let them see that Christ lives because He lives in us. But generally, many times we are perplexed by what is happening in our environment. The changes that happen so fast in the world, and the complexity with which we are presented by world news, social, political, and economical, take us to a new social phenomenon indicating different reactions socially. Fear, for example, because even things that are ours and we desire them with love, seem to be destroyed or lost. There is usually an attitude of apathy to almost all matters around us. As I already mentioned about fear, we can also see an apathetic attitude of positive acceptance that comes in negative opportunities, but that is because they are accepted by society in general. Then, and gradually, they are introduced into the lives of Christians, ending in the acceptance of such things.

But we Christians should not be afraid of changes, because God has promised to be with us at all times. He will enlighten us to focus on these changes by providing us with the necessary strength to face them. We can see some of these challenges as good opportunities to make the presentation of the gospel.

Chapter 2

Conversations with Dr. Kennedy

I express my gratitude to the Almighty for giving me the opportunity to personally meet Dr. Kennedy (or Jim as we affectionately called him) and have many conversations while I was the International Director of Evangelism Explosion. We always had a very friendly, cordial, brotherly relationship contributing to the fulfillment of evangelization. For him, Christ was the Lord, and he manifested it not only in his preaching, but in his daily life, showing others that Christ lives because he lived in his own life. Many times we went out to deal with administrative matters related to the development of the ministry, but we ended up with conversations about the Lord and his mandate to fulfill the Great Commission. On many occasions we ended up presenting the gospel to someone that God put in our path.

I remember one occasion when he made the diagnostic questions to a lady who attended the table where we were having lunch. She didn't know what to answer because she recognized Dr. Kennedy, and began to confess certain problems. Later Jim, directing the conversation, made the gospel presentation and she accepted the gift of eternal life. Experiences like this were common in my outings with Dr. Kennedy. We usually had lunch at a restaurant not far from the church.

Sometimes we walked to the beach and always made the presentation of the gospel to someone. God always provided us with the famous "divine appointments." Sometimes he started the presentation and then in the middle of the conversation, he asked me to end the conversation. We usually ended up with some new Christians. Many of them came to the Coral Ridge Church, as it was a well-known church in the city of Fort Lauderdale.

Jim was frank, loyal, sincere and consecrated. He made the greatest sacrifices in the exercise of his mission in fulfilling the Great Commission and his interest in training other brothers to comply with the mandate of our Lord Jesus.

There were times when, in the privacy of his office, we entered into valuable theological conversations. We wondered if the church regarded the world as if it were ready for the gospel, and Jim thought this was so, that the church has always believed that the world is ready for the Gospel. Naturally, I agree with him. I think the failure of winning the world for Christ usually is attributed not to the situation where the world is but to the failure of the church to take on the task of evangelization. That is why we are interested in expanding the ministry of Evangelism Explosion to reach all nations. And we were able to reach more than 200 nations in the world.

This certainty about seeing the world as ready for evangelization has been very marked. It has been continuous, being a very clear and just conviction for the church. The church has been right to be sure that the world is always ready for the gospel. I think this has been quite clear in the contemporary missionary movement. For example, we see it very clearly in the situation with Japan. For many years Japan was ruled by military forces that were against the United States, but once the missionary effort arrived in Japan after World War II, things changed. (Evangelism Explosion is very present in Japan now.)

Whether countries are ready for the gospel depends not only on external things, but also on internal affairs, on the heart of man. Naturally, the disposition of the world to receive the message of salvation depends greatly on the intervention of the Holy Spirit, who touches the heart of man. That is why when we make the presentation of the gospel to strangers, we have to do it with the assurance of the presence of the Holy Spirit in our presentation. He is the one who attracts to Himself in the famous divine encounters we saw on the beach or in restaurants in Fort Lauderdale, and elsewhere.

Dr. Kennedy believed that the disposition of the world depended on God alone. In this we were in complete agreement. The fundamental principle is that the willingness of the world to receive the salvific message depends solely on God. It is very difficult to find another biblical teaching than this one because God is the center of everything related to evangelization and everything that revolves around us. He prepares people. He is the one who directs the planting and harvesting. The developments of history do not control it, He controls it. Because of all this is that there are always opportunities for evangelization. God is the one who controls the universe and is the one who directs the mission of His Church. Because of His continued participation is that He always provides opportunities for evangelization.

I remember Dr. Kennedy saying that our needs were not just for food, medicine, and education. There was another type of need, the most basic of them: the need to receive Christ as Savior. It is because of this need that man is ready. There is no substitute for this need and that is why the whole world is ready for evangelization. Do we believe that man without Christ is lost? Do we believe that man desperately needs the salvation that is in Christ? Do we believe that there is no other name under heaven that can save us? If we believe this, then we must also believe that the world is ready and must respond in missionary obedience.

Dr. Kennedy mentioned that for us to reach the hearts of the people around us we must be very committed to the presentation of the message of life. And Evangelism Explosion would be the answer for many leaders everywhere.

Jim always quoted Dr. Charles Robinson, professor of Theology at the Columbia Presbyterian Seminary, where Jim and I had the blessing to receive our first theological degrees. Although several years after Jim, I did my Theology studies in this Seminary. Dr. "Robi", as we affectionately called him, was our Professor of Theology.

Dr. Kennedy quoted him frequently, he appreciated him a lot. In fact, one of the classrooms of the Seminary founded by Dr. Kennedy (the John Knox Evangelical Seminary) was named after Dr. Charles Robinson. In a conversation we had about missions Dr. Kennedy said: "As Dr. Robi said: 'the interest in the theology of missions was not directly in the seminaries and theologians but in the missionary circles, and agencies. That is why it is very important," said Dr. Kennedy, "that in the ministry of Evangelism Explosion we included the leaders who led these mission boards."

The church presents the essential antidote for sin and for the lack of unity that exists among the people of God which is one of the consequences of sin. Adam's sin led man to oppose the Creator. After it brought the result of the murder of Abel and created the disunity we see in the Tower of Babel. Yes, sin brings disunity, conflict between Christians and a moving away from the Creator. It is the Incarnation and Redemption of the Lord that destroys the separation created between man and God. This is why Dr. Kennedy's emphasis on training, equipping of each Christian in how to make the presentation of the gospel was like the "bread" of each day.

The church is the "new creation" heir of the promises made by our Lord to the people of Israel. It is the body of which Christ is the source of unity, and is the head; which is the temple of which He is the cornerstone. Because of this we can see the continued presence of Christ among us. Therefore, it has been called to carry out the mission: *"Peace be with you! As the Father sent me, so I am sending you"* (John 20:21). *"Therefore go and make disciples of all the nations, baptizing them in the name of the Father and of the Son and of the Holy Spirit, and teaching them to obey everything I have commanded you; and, I surely I am with you always, to the very end of the age"* (Matt. 28:19-20). The reception from men is identified with Christ: *"Whoever listens to you listens to me; and whoever rejects you, rejects me, but whoever rejects me, rejects him who sent me."* (Luke 10:16).

The church is very necessary for salvation. It exists to allow all men to share the grace of salvation brought to us by the Redemption in the expansion of the kingdom of Christ throughout the world. It is in itself salvation because it carries with it the saving message for humanity, the continuous presence of the Savior. In the conversations I had with Dr. Kennedy, we confirmed that it would be very difficult for man to face the church in opposition to the fulfillment of the Great Commission. Dr. Kennedy was totally convinced, as I am, that our evangelizing task depends on the continued presence of Christ among us. It is the Holy Spirit that testifies to our spirit that we are children of God. He is here to help and guide us in this evangelizing task.

Being close to Christ, confessing him as our Savior, being effective and actively participating in the Church, is a single matter. We could say, (as we said in Lares where I was born), it's all the same.

It was a joy to be with Dr. Kennedy because he lived this whole thing. I remember on one occasion, when he presented the gospel to a person who was a "divine appointment", when he made the second diagnostic question ("Imagine that you die and you present yourself before God and He asks you: Why should I let you in my heaven? What would you say?") Dr. Kennedy spoke these words not as something intellectual but with words that flowed from his heart, which was clearly seen as he looked at the person, in his "nonverbal" communication. Yes, Dr. Kennedy, at the moment of presenting the gospel, let the Holy Spirit to clearly manifest in their conversation. I learned a lot from this great teacher for which I am very grateful to God.

Every time we went out with Dr. Kennedy, although we talked about administrative matters, to solve some problems, the most important thing for us was the presentation of the gospel if God provided the opportunity, to make the presentation of Evangelism Explosion. Generally, after making the presentation of the gospel we made a short evaluation of the presentation. I always had at my disposal a notebook with a pen ready to take notes, because, for me, these meetings were special classes to improve our presentation of the gospel.

I remember on one occasion, just days before the celebration of 25 years of ministry of Evangelism Explosion, which we celebrated at the First Baptist Church of Fort Lauderdale, one of the visitors, brother Dr. Theo Kunst, from Belgium asked him a question: "Dr. Kennedy, who can present Christ?" (Of course, this question had the intention of starting a dialogue for the benefit of the participants.) Dr. Kennedy simply said:

"We can all do it; any Christian filled with the Holy Spirit can do it. A believer becomes a witness when he communicates his knowledge of Christ to others so that they too can know Him. Each Christian is called to be a witness and some can be very effective in winning souls, and others will have other experiences. As we make the presentation of the gospel, a burning desire is created in the Christian to continue fulfilling the Great Commission. You need to be alert and prepared to make the presentation at any time, where the Lord provides the opportunity."

We read in the Bible that God's plan for us is that we be witnesses and soul winners. Christ said clearly that his followers should go and make disciples. God has chosen to work through the church; we have to take the initiative in responding to the guidance of the Holy Spirit. We should not wait for people to come to us and ask us to make the presentation of the gospel. This is why Dr. Kennedy was ready, waiting for God to present opportunities "divine appointments" at any time.

I was occupying the position of International Director of Evangelism Explosion for two years and each day was a living experience of God's presence helping us in our responsibilities, training and empowering the Church for the fulfillment of the Great Commission.

While I assumed the responsibilities of the general Directorship of the ministry, Dr. Freddie Estrada Adorno came to take the place of the Vice Presidency of Evangelism Explosion for Latin America. Although Freddie only served for a short time (since his denomination called him to assume other denominational responsibilities) he came to do a good job. Later the governing body of Evangelism Explosion asked me to continue as Vice President of E.E. for Latin America, work that I carried out until the time of my retirement that was made official during the celebration of a Seminary in Fiji in 2012.

Chapter 3

Team of EE Latin America - Panorama

Although some leaders, team members of Evangelism Explosion Latin America, will contribute to writing the story of E.E. in their regions, I want to take the liberty to review each region to help a little to explain the story of E.E. Latin America.

The first team that God brought to collaborate in the beginning and development of E.E. in the continent of Latin America was composed by Dr. Osvaldo C. Casati, (Baptist) Director for the Southern Cone; Rev. Mark Searing (Christian and Missionary Alliance) Director for Ecuador and Peru; Rev. Roberto Searing (Christian and Missionary Alliance) Director for Colombia and Venezuela; Rev. David Gomez (Central American Church) Director for the Ministry to Ethnic Groups; Rev. Orlando Álvarez, Director for Central America; Bishop Joel Mora Peña, Director for Mexico. (Later Nahúm Vega took the place of Bishop Mora in Mexico). Brother Will Rodríguez, Director for the Caribbean; Rev. Edwin Gant, Director for the Hispanic People of the United States. (Later this task was shared with Rev. Ray Castro). Mr. Pablo Reus was initially the Director for the Iberian Peninsula, then the direction of this region passed into the hands of Rev. Juan Diego Vallejos in Barcelona.

Such immense work, such as organizing a continental ministry, could never have been the function of just one person. I was always in prayer before the Lord asking that He would provide the appropriate people, with wise and dedicated leadership, to launch the work that God had put in my hands, the organization of the ministry of Evangelism Explosion in our Latin America.

In those first years of the beginning of our ministry, I remember that I received a request for information about the E.E. Hispanic ministry from Rev. Ray Castro, one of the pastors of the "PEOPLES CHURCH" in Fresno, California. He was very interested in knowing about our plans, because he had learned of my new responsibility and participation as new team member of Evangelism Explosion International under the leadership of Dr. Kennedy and Dr. Archie Parrish.

The senior pastor of the Peoples Church, Dr. Johnson, had participated in one of the first clinics held in the "Coral Ridge Presbyterian Church" under the instruction of Dr. Kennedy and Dr. Archie Parrish. Upon their return to Fresno, they began teaching E.E. in their church and was of great interest because of the marked growth of membership in the congregation. The success was so great that they had to employ a pastor to take care of the growth that was emerging from the implementation of E.E. in the church. This pastor was brother Rev. Ray Castro. The ministry of E.E. in that church became one with more growth in the congregation.

Naturally Ray, of Mexican background and knowing Spanish, was very interested in helping us at the beginning of the ministry in our beautiful Latin America. The "Peoples Church" provided scholarships to bring pastors and leaders from Latin America to be trained in the clinics.

In the first group of sponsored students we had 14 pastors and leaders, several from Mexico, others from Puerto Rico, Colombia and Hispanics in the United States. Two of the participants were a couple from Guadalajara, brother Nahum Vega and his first wife Lydia. They were the pioneers of this ministry in Mexico. They began E.E. in Mexico in their church in Guadalajara where brother David Arévalo was pastor. Years later, Nahum became part of our work team for the continent with responsibilities as E.E. Director for Mexico.

Then we had some other clinics at the Peoples Church in Fresno and brother Ray Castro was the one who coordinated them, together with a good team that was available to him as part of the church staff in Fresno.

I extended an invitation to brother Ray to join me as a "work team" to teach in clinics on the continent. He spoke some Spanish, and with practice became one of the best clinic teachers we've had on the continent. He talked about the experience of having started E.E. in the

"Peoples Church" in Fresno with a very marked success of work, also his great interest and dedication in the ministry. God made Ray my ministry partner for eleven years. With him we introduced the ministry in almost all of Latin America, as in Spain and Portugal.

God prepared a work team for the development of the ministry of E.E. on the continent in a very special way. He chose leaders with passion for evangelization of the continent. Each was marked by certain characteristics found in the description of the disciples chosen by the Master to begin His ministry in the Holy Land. They are co-authors of this book that we present here; they have written the story of the beginning and development of E.E. in their respective areas of responsibility.

I merely mention members of the work team by areas of responsibilities, although they, being the Work Team of E. E. Latin America, contributed greatly to the development of ministry outside their areas of responsibilities by creating work strategy, teaching clinics, helping and directing the transitions of materials for a cultural adaptation. We met several times each year to make our plans, which were always soaked in prayer and under the direction of our Heavenly Father, our DIRECTOR.

Let us start with the region known as CONO SUR- Southern Cone (Argentina, Paraguay, Chile, Uruguay and Peru). We started out with brother Dr. Osvaldo César Casati (who already went to be with the Lord). Dr. Casati was used by God in several areas of ministry, who God marked as a special leader for the ministerial responsibilities to which He had called him.

I met Osvaldo when I was working with LOGOI ministry in the years 1974-1976. I was part of the organization of the "Logoi Pastoral Seminars" and where Osvaldo also participated as one of the key leaders. We met for the first time in Santiago, Chile when we went to participate in seminars in the Temuco area. (There we also met brother Pepe Mardóñez and Pastor Rodolfo Campos, leaders of the Christian and Missionary Alliance church in Chile and who contributed greatly in the beginning of E.E. in Chile).

God allowed me to know Osvaldo well because He had very special plans in the near future, to bring Osvaldo as part of our team for Evangelism Explosion in Latin America. God permitted us to know

16

each other, almost like Jonathan and David. Osvaldo became the special key to introduce E.E. in Argentina, Paraguay, Uruguay, Peru and Chile with the great help of a dear and beloved brother, Roberto Jarzack, who was also used by God to contact several key leaders in the area. God used these two brothers with courage and gentleness, and a special love for training and empowering lay leaders in the region.

One of the first E.E. clinics that we organized in the Southern Cone took place in the Baptist Church of Godoy Cruz where brother Dr. Ernesto Humeniuk was pastor, who later became one of the representatives of the continent in the International Body of Directors of Evangelism Explosion, position that was also occupied by Dr. Pablo Méndez, from Colombia.

It is important to mention that during the first E.E. clinic in Argentina I met several key leaders, whom God had already chosen or predestined to take a very active part in the ministry. Sister María Ester de Garay was a person who helped in a special way the development of E.E. in "La Ballena" Baptist Church in Miami, Florida with the Rev. Jorge Comezañas. He then contributed in a special way to the development of E.E. in Spain and Portugal.

I also met, who by then was the President of the Baptist Convention of Argentina, Pastor Dr. Juan Calcagni, who was also the President of one of the branches of Dos Ríos bank. Juan had pastoral responsibilities at the "Christ" Baptist Church of Lanús. God led me to make a special invitation to brother Juan Calcagni to attend a clinic of E.E. in Puerto Rico. Then, following the direction of the Holy Spirit, brother Ray Castro and myself challenged Juan to leave his bank job and devote full time to the pastorate. We knew that if he implemented E.E. in his church, he would have to leave the bank and devote full time to the pastoral ministry. It happened this way, because when he returned from participating in the clinic in Puerto Rico, he began training leaders in his church, which had a very strong growth and became one of the fastest growing Baptist Churches in the city. Juan had to give up work at the Bank and dedicate himself full-time as pastor of the "Christ" Baptist Church of Lanús.

In his congregation as Pastor, Juan trained brother Alfonso Cubillas, to whom the congregation had chosen as Director of E.E. The growth of the congregation was such that they had to open another meeting place where another congregation was organized, in which the brother Alfonso Cubillas became the pastor. Both congregations became bases for clinics. And both congregations remain active in evangelization today.

Osvaldo was dedicated to the development of ministry in such a way that several churches in Argentina began using E.E. with a marked success of growth. One of them was an Assemblies of God Church in the Florida neighborhood where brother Juan Crudo was pastor. I remember one Sunday, after I had preached in this church and made a formal introduction of the ministry of Evangelism Explosion, Pastor Crudo invited me to lunch and then go to a nearby park and enjoy what I thought was a "break". While in the park Pastor Crudo said: "I would like to see in practice what you told us this morning. Could you make the presentation of the Gospel to someone so I can see Evangelism Explosion in action?"

We approached a group of people playing "bochas" (a game where heavy iron balls are tossed within a circle, to achieve points and win). I had never played this game, but anyway I tossed the balls and managed to make some good points. Then one of the players asked me what I did for a living and naturally I told them that I was a pastor and was there with brother Crudo. Then I had the great opportunity to start a dialogue with some of them where I could make the presentation of the Gospel and eight people accepted the gift of eternal life. I remember when I asked the question: Have you reached the point in your life when you have the assurance that if you die today you will go to heaven? There was intrigue in them, concern, but also interest, so I could make the presentation. After accepting the gift of eternal life, they asked me who would help them, to which I replied without hesitation: "Here is Pastor Crudo; I am sure he will help you."

Then we approached a couple who were relaxing on a park bench. After a short presentation I asked if they visited any church and was told that "once in a while they went to one in the neighborhood." I asked them if they were married, to which they replied: "we live together," but with great respect. Then I had the opportunity to make a presentation of the Gospel and they accepted the "gift of Eternal Life". That afternoon pastor Crudo said: "I want all my leaders to be trained in this ministry of Evangelism Explosion." He made arrangements for some (about 20 leaders) to go to the next clinic in Chile where Ray

Castro and I were the clinic teachers. Others were trained in Argentina. This church had a marked growth and used E.E. to start other churches in the country and elsewhere. God gave me the opportunity to preach in some of these churches.

When I was in Temuco, Chile, after having started the clinic and directing the prayer groups, I got a strong "appendix" attack, preventing me from continuing the classes. Ray Castro, who was the other clinic teacher, had to take over the activities, naturally with Osvaldo, Pepe Mardóñez and brother Jarkzack. They called a doctor who turned out to be an obstetrician from one of the maternity clinics, as there was no other doctor available at the time. He came to the door of the hotel room where I was staying and found me rolling around on the floor, suffering severe pains. He said: "This is appendicitis and we have to do surgery immediately". Unfortunately, at that time there were no beds available in the few hospitals in Temuco. After having called several places, the only place that had an available bed was the German Maternity Clinic, where women went to have their babies. I was taken there with my doctor, the Obstetrician, that was taking care of me. There I was a couple of days.

While I was among the patients in that place, hearing their cries during delivery, I had the opportunity to make the presentation of the gospel to twelve of them. All accepted the gift of eternal life. I remember a young man who came to visit his wife and as I approached from the front, as I was walking, doing exercises ordered by the physician, he was laughing. I told him: "You are laughing because you've never seen a man as a patient at this place! Well, let me tell you that yesterday I had a girl ... (because the students of the E.E. Clinic had visited me with brother Ray and had brought a doll just to have a good time). Then I asked him if he ever visited a church there in Temuco. He said yes, but only occasionally. I made the E.E. presentation and he accepted the gift of Eternal Life.

It was a good experience; which God gave me in those moments where several people accepted the gift of Eternal Life. It was also a great lesson for the brothers who participated in the Evangelism Explosion Clinic. They never forgot those positive moments in Temuco.

Osvaldo, with the help of his own team of the Southern Cone, with

Juan Calcagni, Dr. Ernesto Humeniuk, Roberto Jarkzack and other leaders, extended the work training E.E. in the entire country of Argentina, and the other Southern Cone countries, organizing clinics to train leaders that God has used in a very special way.

By the end of 1983 we celebrated an "E.E. CONGRESS" in the city of Córdoba, Argentina with the participation of more than 300 people, who already implemented the E.E. ministry in their local churches with marked success. Brother Ray Castro was one of the speakers together with Juan Calcagni, Osvaldo, pastors and key leaders who had experienced a very marked success in the implementation of the ministry in the country of Argentina.

Brothers Osvaldo C. Casati and John Calcagni have been awarded an Honorary Doctorate in Practical Theology (Honoris Causa Doctorate) by the Online Knox Theological Seminary.

After brother Osvaldo retired, Dr. Guillermo DiGiovanna assumed the responsibility as Regional Director for the Southern Cone for a while. Though he is not the Director at present, he continues helping the brothers who are currently responsible for the development of the ministry in the region. Almost all of Guillermo's help has been under the new administration of Evangelism Explosion Latin America with the new Vice President, Will Rodriguez.

It should be mentioned that Dr. DiGiovanna has been heavily involved in the beginnings of the project of the Online Knox Theological Seminary, starting to help pastors and leaders on the continent to finish their theological studies. Currently, Guillermo is the President of the Seminary.

The introduction of the ministry of E.E. in Paraguay was the result of the work of brother Bishop Monzón, of the Free Methodist Church, who on his return from the first clinic in Godoy Cruz in Argentina began the work among the Free Methodist brothers. It was not received with great joy, but it did have a slow start. But God has his own plans involving the Mennonite brothers with brother Glassen, who participated in the first clinic in Asunción. The Mennonite brothers began the work with great success, having several clinic bases among their churches. Also, Pedro Berardo, a Baptist pastor, implemented the ministry with great success and his church became a place to continue training other pastors.

From the Southern Cone region, we move over to the region of Brazil where the E.E. ministry was introduced by a Lutheran missionary family, Rev. John Abel, his wife Rubi and his family who belonged to the "American Lutheran Church". Brother John Abel, and his wife Rubi, while developing their work responsibilities to raise funds for their mission in the United States participated in an E.E. clinic. John wanted to be trained in this ministry to later introduce it in Brazil.

John says that on his return to continue his missionary responsibilities in the city of Curitiba, he implemented the ministry starting with a small group of brothers. They were so successful that other pastors wanted to be equipped in E.E. and thus they continued involving other pastors and leaders even though they had not yet completed the official translation of E.E. materials to Portuguese. John and his family did what they could to offer a "homemade" translation of the E.E. materials so that they could continue with the training work for the Lutheran pastoral brothers in Curitiba and elsewhere.

John was the instrument God used to arrange translation of the first edition of materials directly from English to Portuguese. He made contact with the head pastor of the Ipanema Baptist Church, who along with his wife knew good English. I don't remember their names, but I think the pastor's name was "Dapashion." He was the one who made the first translation of the E.E. materials in 1984-5 under the direction of John and David Abel. A little later we had the great help of brother Joaquim de Paula Rosa, who at that time was the director of the Baptist Publications House in Río de Janeiro. Joaquim also served as director of evangelism in the Baptist church of Niteroi where Dr. Nelson Fanini was pastor, a great evangelist.

The First Baptist Church of Niteroi was one of the first to implement the ministry of E.E. with marked success. They hold clinics every year which are very successful. They trained thousands of pastors and leaders with the interest of expanding the Kingdom of God in Brazil. On one occasion Dr. Fanini was a special guest of Dr. Kennedy to participate in an E.E. clinic in Coral Ridge, and also was a speaker at one of the special activities of E.E. in Fort Lauderdale, Florida.

Another of the pioneer churches in the introduction of E.E. in Brazil was the "Iglesia Bautista do Brooklyn" in São Paulo. The pastor at that time was Rivas Bretones, along with Joelcio Barreto and other leaders, who participated in a clinic in Fort Lauderdale, Florida. They came back with the idea of implementing the ministry in their local churches and did so with marked success. The first clinic carried out in Brazil was conducted in the "Iglesia Bautista do Brooklyn", where Ray Castro and I were the clinic teachers. Pastor Joelcio Barreto, together with David Abel, were the translators.

A key leader who participated in this clinic was Dr. Georgie Caniellas of the Presbyterian Church of Brazil. He was used by God to introduce E.E. among the brothers of the United Presbyterian Church in Brazil, being one of the pastors in a central church in Sao Paulo. Then he came to be the head pastor at the Presbyterian Church of Villa Maria (Presbyterian Church of Brazil) where he has continued his pastoral work. There began E.E. with great success and then became a "clinic base". Many evangelical leaders were trained in those clinics. Another leader I want to mention was pastor Carlos Alberto Brito Braz and his wife Ida Katherine Andeston Braz, who participated in the same church with Caniellas for several years. Then they went to assume the head pastorate of a new congregation where E.E. was successfully implemented which then became a clinic base.

The region of Brazil has been shared by three members of the E.E. Latin America Work Team. The first Director was brother John Abel, then his son, David Abel helped in some ways. As we have already said, they were the pioneers in the beginning of E.E. in Brazil. They organized clinics in several places. By November 1985 John Abel sent the following schedule of clinics:

June	6-11	Curitiva, PR	Methodist Church
June	13-18	Campos, RJ	Baptist Church
July	25-30	Belem, PA	Los Hemanos Church
September	5-10	S. Paulo	Brooklyn Baptist Church
October	24-29	S. Paulo	Pres. Church do Villa Maria
November	21-26	Victoria, ES.	David Abel, Vila Velba
November	11-15		EE National Congress

Arrangements were made for some national pastors and leaders to attend clinics in the United States. Several were present in clinics at

Coral Ridge, and other churches offered scholarships to bring leaders from Latin America to participate in their clinics, for example the First Baptist Church of Fort Lauderdale, the Second Ponce de León Presbyterian Church in Memphis, Tennessee, the Peoples Church in Fresno and others. Generally, I was the one who translated for the pastors and leaders of Latin America who participated. Some could go to clinics in Spanish in Puerto Rico, but almost everyone participated in clinics in the United States.

After the time of John and David Abel, Dr. José Carlos Ribeiro (who greatly helped in the development of E.E. Brazil until we started the development of the Field Workers project) began to lead the ministry in Brazil.

Sister Alejandra de Jesús (faithful companion of missionary work) began working with the ministry in Brazil because of her interest in the ministry of Evangelism Explosion. She had been trained in Miami by Pastor Edgardo Avero in the congregation that is called today "Ekklesia." The Lord provided the opportunity for her to be an arduous promoter of the Ministry of Evangelism Explosion among the leaders of ministries with children in various churches in Brazil. She became part of the ministry among the Field Workers.

The work done by Dr. José Carlos Ribeiro continued providing the development of the ministry in Brazil. Under his leadership we held the Congress of E.E. in the city of Aguas de Lindoia, in São Paulo. There we had around 400 participants representing various churches around the country. Although the intention was to organize a meeting for "Teachers of Clinics", that event became a "congress" with the participation of the wives of Clinic Teachers and other leaders interested in the evangelization of the country.

The congress was a blessing, marking key moments for the success of the continuous development of E.E. in Brazil. We set up plans and dreams for E.E. Brazil, which were developing in due course. Similar congresses were held in Argentina and other places. Dr. James Kennedy was present in the Congress of the Southern Cone in Mar del Plata, Argentina. In Brazil, Dr. Thomas Stebins, International Director of E.E. was present as one of the speakers for the congress. Together with Tom Stebins there were other representatives of International E.E. cooperating in the direction of congress.

A couple of years later, the work of the regional office began under the direction of brother Robert Foster, who continues to this day as Director of E.E. Brazil. I remember when I interviewed Robert at the airport in Dallas, he asked me the question about where to study Portuguese to go as missionary to Brazil. I told him, "You are going to study Portuguese in Brazil, in the field of work." Robert and Mary Jo moved with their children to Sao Paulo and began working there and also studied Portuguese. It was a great experience for them and also a blessing for E.E. Latin America. Robert has done a great job in the adaptation of the new materials under the direction of the new Vice President for Latin America, Will Rodríguez. Many churches have begun the ministry of Evangelism Explosion under the direction of brother Foster.

A look at region III
(COLOMBIA, VENEZUELA, ECUADOR and PERU)

Let's take a bird's-eye view of what has been done in REGION III (Colombia, Venezuela, Ecuador and Peru).

Because of the growth of the ministry and the interest developed by local churches, we had to divide the responsibilities of the development of ministry in this region. Brother Robert Searing became Director for Colombia and Venezuela and his son, Mark Searing, assumed the responsibility of the development of the ministry in Ecuador and Peru. Both leaders, Robert and Mark, have been professional missionaries with marked success with the Christian and Missionary Alliance.

Dr. Robert Searing along with his wife Margie, were the pioneers in starting E.E. in Colombia and Ecuador. They sent several key leaders to take the training in Puerto Rico and the United States. There were two churches that were very involved with the ministry of E.E. at the beginning. One of them, where brother Robert Searing was, "El Encuentro" Church (of the Christian and Missionary Alliance) and also Puente Largo Church, with Pablo Mendez and Joshua Reyes as pastors.

Another church that successfully implemented the ministry was the Christian Confraternity Tabernacle of Faith Church where Hector Pardo has been pastor. In one of my reports for the E.E. Board of

24

Directors I mentioned that brother David Clippard went with me on that trip as a clinic teacher, and was very involved in the development of E.E. in North America. Then David was the E.E. Vice President for the United States.

When David accompanied me on the trip to Colombia, Venezuela and Ecuador, it was with the intention to share with leaders of these countries about how the ministry of E.E. had been helpful in his church, where he was the pastor in charge of the ministry of evangelism. This was the "Southcliff" Baptist Church in Fort Worth, Texas. My interest in inviting David was to motivate and involve more Southern Baptists, and at the same time, make him challenge the church leaders of third region countries. During that trip we had the opportunity to invite some leaders to participate in the next clinics to be held at Southcliff Baptist Church in Fort Worth. One of the participants was Pastor Horacio Prado Paz, who, on his return to Quito, was the instrument used by God to begin the ministry in that Andean country.

Horacio, who was one of the pastoral leaders in Quito, began training in his local congregation. With effort and direction from E.E. Latin America we got to organize the first clinic in Ecuador where brother Horacio was pastor. We had the participation of some missionary brothers of the P.C.A. and other pastors: Rev. Vicente Viera, Gustavo Molina and J. A. Creamer, who became the leaders of the group organized in Quito.

In Bogotá, Colombia, the contact was brother Héctor Pardo, who became the President of the Contact Committee. The meeting took place in one of the rooms of Bacatá Hotel. Several leaders were present representing different denominations and two organizations, S.E.P.A.L. and World Vision. We organized the National Council of E.E. Advisors with Héctor Pardo as President, Pablo Méndez Nieto, as Secretary and Héctor Machuca, as Vice President. Then some of them participated at the "Peoples Church" Clinic in Fresno, California, as well as in the clinics we had in Puerto Rico at the First Baptist Church in Carolina, and in the Country Club Christian Alliance Church, where brother Carmelo Terranova was the pastor.

In Caracas, Venezuela, the people responsible for organizing the first meeting were brothers Samuel Olson and Santiago Montero, pastors of "Las Acacias" Church. The pastors and leaders who had participated in the ministry of E.E. were invited as special participants. Rev. Sheridan Eck, of the Evangelical Free Church, made the arrangements for us to visit their Seminary in Maracay. They were teaching E.E. in this seminary using a translation of the E.E. book they had done.

It was a good translation effort, even though it did not have official permission from E.E. or Dr. James Kennedy. However, God used this translation in a positive way. We could say that it was a great contribution by the missionaries of the Evangelical Free Church towards the beginning of the great growth that Evangelism Explosion obtained on the continent.

Brother pastor Gonzalo Afanador, from the Foursquare Church, together with Santiago Montero, and Sheridan Eck shared their experiences in the implementation of E.E. in their churches. The enthusiasm was very marked when they told us about the experiences the E.E. teams had in their respective congregations. Everyone had experiences where several people had accepted the gift of eternal life.

We discussed the vision of E.E. for the continent which led us to organize the National Council of E.E. Advisors for Venezuela. Samuel Olson spoke very positively about his experience in the ministry after attending the clinic in Fort Lauderdale. The National Council of Advisors was organized with the participation of the following members:

Rev. Samuel Olson	Las Acacias Church
Rev. Gonzalo Afanador	Foursquare Church
Rev. Gordon Gilmore	Mennonite Church
Rev. Justo Blanco	Evangelical Free Church
Rev. Alvin Fast	World Vision
Rev. Victor Suárez	Independent
Rev. Ramón González	Presbyterian
Rev. Heberto Camacho	Independent
Rev. Valentin Vale	Assemblies of God

We went to the island of Puerto Rico where Pastor Rev. Felix Castro, with arduous interest in evangelization, welcomed us with open arms. In one of my visits with brother Felix (I visited him frequently as he was the pastor who officiated our wedding ceremony for Carmen and me in 1963) I asked him how he had known about the ministry of Evangelism Explosion, he told me: "I have always been very interested in fulfilling evangelization, because it is a command given by God. In the ministry it is not only a matter of preaching from the pulpit, but we have to make the presentation of the gospel from person to person. I obtained almost all the books published in Venezuela about Evangelism Explosion and here they are." He opened a closet and showed me all the books he had acquired in Venezuela; he had bought the entire collection! Each book was well marked by the students during the teachings they had had. He added: "This is what has helped me to raise this congregation of 3,000 members. I hope we can officially begin this ministry in our congregation as soon as possible."

Brother pastor Félix Castro sent several leaders of his congregation to participate in the E.E. clinics in Fort Lauderdale, as well as in other places, as in Fresno, Memphis, etc. Several church leaders were trained in the E.E. and began successfully their ministry at their local church. Then we began to carry out clinics in this church under the direction of pastor José Calo Castro, nephew of brother Felix. There we trained leaders from Latin America and Puerto Rico. I remember that the brothers Juan Calcagni from Argentina and Brother Valentin Vale from Venezuela, along with several leaders of our "Brown" America, were trained in the first clinic we had at this Baptist church in Carolina, Puerto Rico.

I have to mention other churches of Puerto Rico where they implemented the ministry very successfully. The church "Cathedral of Hope", where brother Carmelo B. Terranova was the pastor, (who is already with the Lord) embraced greatly the ministry making the "Cathedral of Hope" a clinic base. But even more, he was a key example so that other pastors of Puerto Rico and outside the island, became interested in this ministry, which was showing the great growth of the church. The testimony of this congregation served as motivation for several pastors from Puerto Rico and elsewhere in order to strive to implement Evangelism Explosion. The result was wonderful, with very marked growth never seen in many of the churches that implemented it. Carmelo, together with Cristino Díaz, José Calo Castro, and Félix Castro were pioneers of Evangelism Explosion ministry in Puerto Rico, and helped other churches in Puerto Rico, the Caribbean and the continent to begin the ministry.

Presbyterian Churches in Mayagüez, Aguadilla, Lares, Isabela, and San Sebastian were churches that for several years trained leaders in the ministry of E.E. Pastor José Luis Torres (Chewi), (who is already with the Lord) dedicated several years implementing the ministry in Aguadilla, at the Third Presbyterian Church congregation. One or two years before the ministry officially began in Puerto Rico, Pastor Rev. Ramón Miranda, at the Third Presbyterian Church of Mayagüez, having known the ministry, dedicated time to train some lay people in his congregation. One of them was brother Will Rodriguez, who eventually continued training and equipping himself in order to take my place as Vice President of E.E. for Latin America.

One church I should mention is the Presbyterian Church of San Sebastián located on this "Island of Enchantment". Pastor Cruz Ginorio, from 1964 to 1965, dedicated time to train several lay people in his congregation, which turned out in good growth among them. Then the pastor left and continued his ministry in the United States leaving Rev. Héctor Nieves as the local pastor, who then moved to Rochester in July 1985. Then brother Rafael Riquelme continued the training of E.E. in the church, who also left the church to assume pastoral responsibilities elsewhere. Then the Rev. José Lugo took the responsibility and continued with the training in this church. Occasionally, brother Lugo visits the United States.

But what is interesting is that the local leaders of the congregation continued the training, turning the church of San Sebastián into a clinic base. This shows us that even though several pastors left this church to assume responsibilities elsewhere, the ministry continued operating due to the interest generated among the lay members of the church. This is why it is very important that the work of training revolve around the Lord's call for the laity, members of the local church, in order to fulfill with evangelization.

Some of the Reformed Christian churches, especially the one of Fair View, Río Piedras, with Pastor Rev. Roberto Rampolla, were places where the ministry of E.E. was implemented with great success. The church of Fair View became a clinic based church, where hundreds of pastors and leaders came to train.

Rev. Cristino Díaz, who was the pastor of the Baptist Church of Río Piedras, one of the most recognized churches in Puerto Rico due to the ministry among university students, implemented the ministry successfully, turning the church into a "clinic base." There were trained leaders from several churches of the island, as well as from Santo Domingo and other places of the continent. I remember the pastor, Rev. Cristino Díaz, who with great interest organized all the details for each clinic we had there. The church used the ministry of Evangelism Explosion with much success for several years.

I think it is important to mention that it was here in Puerto Rico where God marked the standards to select the leaders who would direct the ministry of E.E. in the continent of Latin America. First to myself, Dr. Cecilio Lajara, and the current Vice President, Will Rodriguez, whom God gave me the opportunity to help, guide, and train toward the direction of the ministry at the continental level.

God had chosen brother Will Rodríguez as Director of the Caribbean Region, including the "English Caribbean." He quit his job at the Hewlett Packard International Company, where he received good pay. Will accepted the challenge we made to assume the responsibility of the Directorship of E.E. ministry for the Caribbean, work that had to be done and is still done by faith, without much economic security. I remember those times when Will and his beloved wife Tatita had to make a decision in order to take the responsibility as Director for the Caribbean with an extremely limited salary, in comparison with the possibilities to receive a large sum of money in "commissions" due to equipment sales from the company where he used to work.

I remember that my offer was something miserable, and at the time I offered it I felt like hiding under the table. It was a low salary, which he would have to look for by faith with the expectation that God would provide it in one way or another. But when God touches the heart of a person making a ministerial call, it is not possible to refuse. This was the experience of both Will and Tatita. Will did not receive the big economic gains from the company for which he worked, but they have received even greater profits being servants of the King of Kings as the Vice President of E.E. for Latin America.

An overview of EE development in Cuba

I started going to Cuba in 1998 by faith, because I had no notification from the Cuban Government to be able to enter the communist island. It was by faith and God opened the doors. In my plans to introduce the ministry in Cuba, I made plans with pastor Rev. Gary César and the leaders of Evangelism Explosion of Ciudad Satélite Baptist Church in order to invite some Cuban pastors to participate in the next clinic they were planning. We defined the plans and invited five Cuban pastors to participate in the next clinic. The Baptist Church of Satélite covered all expenses, registration and accommodation of those pastors and church leaders in Cuba.

Only three of the five pastors blessed by the Baptist Church of Ciudad Satélite, implemented the ministry and were blessed for it. Brother Rev. Felipe Rodríguez, pastor of the Baptist Church in Regla started with great enthusiasm and dedication. Their efforts were a blessing to many, especially for the first couple of disciples in training, Israel and Dodani, who at the time were dating.

The church had a marked growth as a result of the implementation of E.E. There we had the first E.E. clinic in Cuba and it was when I met Israel and Dodani, who were leaders in the clinic. The result of the clinic was very successful, as much for the local church there in Regla, and for the churches represented in the clinic.

Several churches began the ministry successfully, many of them became a clinic base. The ministry grew very healthy and clinics were held every month, sometimes up to two clinics per month.

God allowed Israel to become the Director of the ministry on the Island and his participation was very useful for the growth of E.E. in Cuba. Thanks to God we can say that more than 400 churches have implemented this ministry on the Island of Cuba. This was a training and a great coaching for Israel, who also finished his theological studies at the Baptist Seminary in Havana, and has received a couple of doctorates from the Baptist Seminary of Dallas, Texas.

Another leader from the development of E.E. in Cuba has been Rev. Gilberto Corredera, currently pastor of the Hispanic ministries at Prestonwood Baptist Church in Houston, Texas. Gilberto Corredera served in Cuba with the brothers of the Church "Los Pinos Nuevos" and was one of the teachers of the E.E. clinics in Cuba. He was the pioneer of E.E. among the brothers of his denomination, "Los Pinos Nuevos." By joining Israel, they formed a great work team with key leaders. Some of them were doctors, and renounced medicine to dedicate full time to the development of Evangelism Explosion on the Island of Cuba.

Currently, Israel is one of the pastors of the First Baptist Church of Orlando and is in charge of the Hispanic ministries in the congregation.

A Cuban E.E. work team was organized, who continued training and equipping other leaders to fulfill the Great Commission. Thus, the ministry grew with remarkable success with more than 400 churches involved using the evangelistic outreach ministry. This has been a blessing for the churches in Cuba. During the development of E.E. in Cuba, God raised up leaders that today serve the Lord in different parts of the United States and the continent of Latin America.

The ministry was also introduced in the other Caribbean Islands and in Santo Domingo and Haiti with remarkable success. On the Island of Jamaica there was a very marked awakening in the churches that began with E.E. and it was where the clinics were first carried out to train leaders of the other islands, that could only communicate in English, although some could understand a little Spanish and Papiamentu. Jamaica was one of the Islands where a marked growth was shown, under the direction of brother William Childs. Rev. Tim McClain was the first Director for the English Caribbean. Then Will Rodríguez assumed this responsibility.

I remember we made a courtesy visit to Santo Domingo in order to make contacts with some pastors and leaders of some denominations. We contacted brother pastor Grullón, who had attended a clinic at the First Baptist Church of Río Piedras, Puerto Rico. Upon returning to his Christian & Missionary Alliance church in Santo Domingo, he began training leaders in the congregation. The results were a great blessing for the local church as well as for the denomination. God gave them the blessing of becoming a clinic base. There we had the first clinic in Santo Domingo and after that a clinic was held every year. The contribution of brother Grullón was a great blessing, so that many people could accept the gift of Eternal Life in the Dominican Republic.

We also saw a good start in the English Caribbean Islands, as in Jamaica, Trinidad, Tobago and other places. Many of these leaders participated in clinics in Fort Lauderdale as well as in Venezuela and Puerto Rico. One of the first Directors of the region, Tim McClain reported about the good growth in Jamaica.

Central America

We began the ministry in Central America, as in other places, by generating interest in key leaders in the various Central American countries to participate in the Ministry of Evangelism Explosion. Several of them were trained at the Coral Ridge Church, others in Puerto Rico and Santo Domingo, and other churches with base clinics such as the Peoples Church in Fresno, California, the Southcliff Baptist Church in Dallas, the Second Presbyterian Church in Memphis, Tennessee, and so on. Generally, these churches with base clinics offered scholarships for guests.

There was a first effort to introduce the ministry in Costa Rica, with brothers descendants of the Caribbean islands. But it really began when pastor Orlando Álvarez, from the Assemblies of God Church, was trained at Coral Ridge with other brothers from Central America. Orlando began to train the leaders in his congregation, spreading the idea of E.E. development in the country, with the hope of turning the congregation into a center to train other believers in the country. Leaders, such as Dr. Daniel Morales, participated there, who is still involved in the E.E. ministry serving as advisor in some areas of the ministry. Brother Mario Iglesias, after studying at the Theological Seminary SETECA and getting married, serves with his wife Paola as missionaries in Spain.

Orlando's church had a marked growth, which led them to buy the neighboring properties of the church in order to expand the place where they celebrated their Sunday worship service. The growth was very remarkable, and soon became one of the largest churches in the city. There was a group of young leaders that God used greatly in the growth of ministry in the country. Then these young people became leaders in other ministries. I remember being with Daniel Morales, Josué Blanco and Mario Iglesias making plans to start the young project of the Evangelism Explosion ministry. They took the task of translation and adaptation of the E.E. Youth project from English to Spanish. This ministry had a great boom and growth among youth groups of the churches of the continent. This was a great contribution of that church in San José, Costa Rica.

E.E. had its beginnings in Guatemala, the country of the "chapines", with the Presbyterians in Quetzaltenango. Two years before the first clinic took place in Guatemala, it turns out that a Presbyterian missionary had participated in a clinic in the United States and after translating the materials, he implemented them in his ministry. Unfortunately, he had little success because such materials had not been adapted to the culture. Dr. James Kennedy made a short three-day visit to Guatemala in order to be with this missionary and motivate him in his work, but the effort did not achieve much success.

It was until a couple of missionaries from Wycliffe, Edgar and Eleanor Beach, who had taken one of the clinics in the United States, returned to Guatemala, so Edgar could continue his missionary work as a translator of the New Testament to "Tectiteco", one of the indigenous languages of Guatemala. Eventually by 1993, Edgar finished the translation, which was received with much blessing. His wife, Eleanor, dedicated her time to train and equip various leaders in Evangelism Explosion in a local church (Biblia Abierta). One of these leaders was brother David Gómez, whom God had chosen to assume the responsibilities as Director of the Ministry of Evangelism Explosion in Guatemala and then, as Continental Director of the Ministry of Ethnic Groups of Evangelism Explosion in Latin America. Rev. David Gómez became part of the E.E. team for Latin America and continues with these responsibilities.

Several pastors and leaders of several congregations were trained in Evangelism Explosion who implemented the ministry in their congregations. Some of them had marked success, others began but did not finish. Brother Costop, pastor of the Christian and Missionary Alliance, was one of those who worked until he turned his church into a clinic base. Another church that became a clinic base was the "Biblia Abierta" Church where brother David Gómez worked as an assistant. This congregation took the ministry with many efforts and had a remarkable success. David and his wife Irma were the instruments used by God for the success of the ministry.

Several years later this church organized the first clinic for ethnic leaders with the participation of 32 leaders of several indigenous groups. The leader used by God to organize this clinic was pastor David Gómez. Then David, along with sister Eleanor Beach, continued to provide good follow-up to these leaders by supervising and assisting the different translations into indigenous languages. I remember that in that congregation we had a seminar where we invited several key leaders of the different ethnic groups in Guatemala. Also, there was participation by some leaders from Mexico, of the Chol people and the Mayas.

These brothers of different ethnic groups were used by the Lord to make the translations and cultural adaptations to the Evangelism Explosion materials. It has been very valuable to dedicate time to these believers of different ethnicities so they can know about the Savior, because they are also part of the "people of God."

Centuries before Jesus was born in Bethlehem, the prophet Isaiah foretold the birth of the Savior in a notorious way when he wrote: *"For to us a child is born, to us a son is given, and the government will be on his shoulders. And he will be called Wonderful Counselor, Mighty God, Everlasting Father, Prince of Peace." (Isaiah 9:6)* Now this message can be translated and known in many ethnic groups on our continent, from beautiful Latin America thanks to God who has provided brother David and sister Eleanor Beach to lead this ministry with passion and love in Christ.

Thus the ministry of Evangelism Explosion continued its marked, paced development guided by the Lord. In Honduras, Bishop Francisco Ochoa, of the Church of God of Prophecy, was interested in training several of the leaders of his denomination. We made arrangements and some of them were recipients of scholarships from some churches in the United States. Others were trained in clinics in Puerto Rico, Mexico and Guatemala. Bishop Ochoa had so much interest that he went in search of funds in his denomination to make a special publication of the E.E. materials to use with the believers of the Church of God of Prophecy in Honduras. Of course, these materials were a great help in other countries and other denominations, although they had to make some adjustments to the book's introduction, because the reputation of the Church of God of Prophecy was very marked. But it was helpful in expanding the ministry in Central

America.

I remember one occasion when Bishop Ochoa, wanting to know if this ministry could be used among the brothers of the Church of God of Prophecy in Honduras (as it originated and developed in a Reformed church) he wanted us to go on some evangelistic visits. This was the dialogue we had on the first visit, which proved to be a "divine appointment."

"Good morning, I am Cecilio Lajara and I am visiting with Bishop ..."

"Good morning, it is a pleasure to receive you in my house. Come in and take a seat. Mr. Bishop, my sister has told me a lot about you and the congregation, but I am very busy and cannot go to church." (She was a business lady and she said she didn't believe in "nonsense" like her sister.)

I said: "Well, sister Magda, it is about this "nonsense" that we want to talk to you about." I continued with the presentation of the gospel and she became interested when I asked the question: "Have you gotten to the point in your life when you have the assurance that if you die today you will go to heaven?" (We didn't know she had a car accident the previous week; she told us about her experience and how she was near death.)

"That is why it is extremely important, sister Magda, that we know about the 'nonsense' that your sister knows. Just as God protected you in your accident, He continues to protect you today and always. Now let me ask another simple question: If you had died in that accident, and when you got to heaven God had asked you: Why should I let you into my heaven? What would you have answered?

Of course, her answer was "by works" from her contributions to the Catholic Church and some aids, etc. God gave me the opportunity to continue making the presentation of the gospel, and she accepted the "gift of Eternal Life" ... Then I invited the bishop to pray.

The bishop, very silent and watching everything, later said: "I want you to train all the leaders in my church and in our denomination here in Honduras and throughout Central America." It was a glorious experience and which the bishop always made reference to when speaking of Evangelism Explosion.

Thus, the ministry of Evangelism Explosion entered Honduras and I can say that this was my experience throughout "Brown" America, so that I express my deep gratitude to our Lord and Savior.

In Panama pastor Roberto Bruneau, of the Baptist Church "de la Boca" was one of the first Panamanians trained in E.E. and helped to introduce the ministry of E.E. in the country along with some Baptist missionaries. After several efforts, Roberto could train some brothers with the help of the Southern Baptist missionaries who dedicated time for this work. These missionaries also began the training at the First Baptist Church of Panama with pastor Rev. James D. Watson, who had great success in his efforts. We had a clinic where we trained several leaders and pastors of local churches, but the ministry did not have the same emphasis and projection as in other Central American countries. After a few years, several leaders were trained in clinics in Costa Rica, including brother Ángel Mena. Then the Foursquare denomination took a good leadership by training leaders of various denominations. There were several training clinics among them and brother Mena greatly helped the brothers in Panama. The pastor Orlando Álvarez was a great blessing by coaching and training Panamanians in his church in San José, Costa Rica.

The ministry began in Nicaragua with an introductory visit from our office in Fort Lauderdale. That first meeting was organized by the Cuban brother, Rev. Pastor Tamayo, pastor of First Baptist Church in Managua. Then other churches such as the Canaan Baptist Church in Managua, whose pastor was brother Miguel Rivera Alvarado, got involved by training a good number of members as well as believers of other nearby congregations.

Several years of E.E. training passed when pastor Rev. Sofonías Chávez assumed the responsibility as Coordinator of the ministry, continuing to train and teach countless pastors and leaders. Sofonías became a member of the Central America E.E. Team and continues with these responsibilities. When we organized the "Field Workers" teams, he was an active part of this work team in Evangelism Explosion.

We started the Ministry of Evangelism Explosion in Mexico almost at the beginning when I became part of Dr. Kennedy's work team. It was precisely in 1980 when I made my first trip to Mexico in order to share with my friends and other leaders about the Ministry of Evangelism Explosion.

We made the invitation to several brothers to participate in some of the clinics that were held only in English at that time, because the translation of the materials had not been finished. I remember I had to serve as a translator in some of the clinics. At that time, we only brought pastors and leaders to the clinics at the Coral Ridge Church in Fort Lauderdale, the Peoples Church, in Fresno, California; the Second Ponce Presbyterian in Memphis, Tennessee; the First Baptist Church in Fort Smith, Kansas; the Central Church in Memphis, Tennessee, the Methodist Church in Carrollton, Texas and others. All these churches provided scholarships, including travel expenses, with the purpose of extending the ministerial help of Evangelism Explosion.

I remember that for several years, the Methodist Church in College Station, Texas, dedicated all its missionary efforts to introduce the ministry of Evangelism Explosion to Mexico. The pastor, who at that time was Rev. Terry Tekel and his assistant Randy Wimpee made several trips to Monterrey, Mexico in order to explore and expand their missionary vision with the Methodists believers in Mexico, especially in Monterrey, where the Methodist churches had begun the ministry with much success under the leadership of Bishop Joel Mora Peña and the pastor of the Methodist Church "La Trinidad", Rev. Elías Díaz. The leader of evangelism was brother Joel Ordaz.

The Methodist Church in College Station, Texas took the responsibility of all the expenses, including the introduction of Evangelism Explosion in Mexico. They began covering the salaries of the people involved in the ministry in this country, and provided a new vehicle. They also covered the office expenses, including travel expenses of the Regional Director, who by then was bishop Joel Mora Peña.

Under the leadership of brother Joel Mora Peña, the ministry was introduced in all Methodist churches in northern Mexico and other congregations. The Presbyterians of Monterrey, as in other nearby cities, also captured the vision and got involved in training and equipping their members. Some of these churches became clinic bases, such as the Presbyterian church of Tampico.

The ministry had a great start and development in Monterrey. Then bishop Joel Mora Peña accepted a pastoral call to one of the northern cities of Monterrey, resigning his position in Evangelism Explosion. It was then that the engineer, Nahum Vega Orozco was invited to assume the responsibility of Director of E.E. Mexico and continues with these responsibilities today.

Nahúm Vega was responsible for the direction of the ministry of Evangelism Explosion and was a member of the Church "Centro Cristiano Juan 14: 6" where brother Rev. David Arévalo was pastor. At that time, Nahúm worked at the Guadalajara airport as one of the air traffic controllers. I remember when I made the invitation to brother Nahúm, I did not expect that he would even consider it, because the pay was very limited compared to what he received as an engineer in the air control tower at the Guadalajara airport. But to my surprise, his response was very positive and he said he would think about it and pray with his first wife, sister Lydia (who went to be with the Lord a few years later).

Nahúm assumed the responsibilities as the Director of Evangelism Explosion of Mexico in 1983. God also blessed brother Nahúm in a spectacular way by providing him with a new wife, sister Cristi, who has assumed a very good responsibility as wife and helper in the ministry. Sister Cristina has been Director of the E.E. Ministry of Children in Mexico and has been a great contribution to the ministry on the continent. Currently, she continues cooperating and helping with this ministry.

As I mentioned before, the ministry in Mexico served as a springboard to begin ministry in the communist country of Cuba. Since several churches of different denominations began ministry with marked success in Mexico, the First Baptist Church of Satélite with its pastor Rev. Gary Cesar and Nahúm planned to provide scholarships so that Cuban pastors and leaders could go to Mexico and participate in the clinic programed to take place at the First Baptist Church of Satélite. Plans were confirmed by the churches of Cuba and five Cuban pastors received the scholarships offered by this church in Mexico. This was the beginning of the introduction of the ministry in Cuba that later developed very successfully.

Spain

After reviewing the results of our ministry in the Latin American Continent, let's approach the mother country, Spain, or as we used to call the region: "The Iberian Peninsula." My first visit to Spain was a result of the interest of some leaders (Rev. Juan Blake of the Billy Graham team, Rev. Fernando Vangioni, also of the Billy Graham team but with pastoral responsibilities in Madrid, a personal friend Dr. David Estrada from Barcelona, also Rev. Carlos Gómez and others). Some of them wrote requesting information about Evangelism Explosion. I met them with the hope of organizing a work team and start Evangelism Explosion in the Iberian Peninsula.

We organized a contact group in Spain, the National Council of Advisers, and began with the development of E.E. Spain. Several of those brothers had the opportunity to come to the United States in order to participate in some Evangelism Explosion clinics in Fort Lauderdale (Coral Ridge), Memphis, Tennessee, the Second Presbyterian, and the People's Church in Fresno, California.

When they returned to Spain they started training under our guidance. Some of the churches had a marked success and then we organize the first E.E. clinic held at the Evangelical Church of Canillejas of F.I.E.I.D.E., where Rev. Roque Sánchez was the pastor, and his son José Pablo Sánchez. I remember we had 65 participants from various churches in Spain. Among them, there were brothers: Rev. Miguel Llagostera, Rev. Seisdedos, Mr. José Pablo Reus, Rev. Juan Blake and others, who later became leaders of the continuous development of Evangelism Explosion in Spain.

Another church that had a marked success in the implementation of the ministry was the Biblia Abierta church, also in Canillejas where Rev. Rodolfo Loyola was pastor. Pedro Pablo Reus, our first Director of E.E. Spain, was a member of this congregation and was one of the persons responsible for the development of the ministry among the believers.

One of the experiences that God has presented to me and had marked the ministry in my life was the moment when we programmed a seminar to train Teachers of Clinics at the Monastery of San Juan de la Cruz in Segovia. This training was in 1985 and we expected the participation of candidates for Teachers of Clinics from several countries in Europe.

Unfortunately, there was a winter storm in those days, which paralyzed almost all Spain and other places. My flight arrived in Madrid extremely late. Brother Pedro Pablo picked me up at the Madrid airport, and we started the long journey to get to Segovia, which was very difficult due to the winter storm. We arrived at 3:00 a.m. the next day.

Upon my arrival at the Monastery of San Juan de la Cruz, a parish priest received us, and said to me: "Ah, you must be the Chief who comes to share the teachings. I have a special cell for you. I'm going to take you to the cell where San Juan De La Cruz lived." We walked the long hallways of the Monastery and arrived at the "cell of San Juan de la Cruz." The parish priest said: "Here you have a little cot, but this one (pointing to a stone bed) is the bed where San Juan de la Cruz slept. I hope you get used to it."

It was a very special experience for me, because during my studies at high school, in Aguadilla, Puerto Rico I had read all the books written by San Juan de la Cruz and Santa Teresita de Jesús. I had the blessing of being able to experience some of them being there in the cell where they were written by their author. The experience was spectacularly spiritual for me; therefore, I express my gratitude to the Almighty.

After two days of being there and during lunch time, the parish priest approached the table and placed in front of me a bottle of a 42-year aged liquor. The parish priest's father had given it to him the first day he entered the Monastery. He put it in front of me saying: "I have saved this whiskey for a person that I like. Since I saw you last night, you are that person. Enjoy it."

I don't drink liquor and the bottle of whisky remained on the table. The priest walked away down the hall, but looking back at me, to see when I was going to open the bottle. Then he approached me and said: "What kind of people are you, that haven't opened the bottle?" Then, standing up and putting my arm over his shoulders, I said: "Let's walk down this hallway and I will explain why I haven't opened the bottle." As we walked, I was blessed to make the gospel presentation using Evangelism Explosion. It was a wonderful experience. I remember that when I made the diagnostic questions, he replied: "Well, that's why I'm here at the monastery."

While we were walking, we approached the chapel. Then he said to me: "We can pray in the chapel." So, we went in and prayed there. He accepted the gift of Eternal Life. Then, after I finished the training for the Teachers of Clinics of Europe, I returned to Fort Lauderdale and continued with my responsibilities from the international office.

After about ten years I had the opportunity to return again to Segovia, Spain, but this time with the Ministry of Sola Fide International. It was my responsibility to teach in a Seminar about Missions for pastors and church leaders in Madrid. Arriving in Segovia, one of the pastors approached me; he had come to the seminar and asked me: "Are you the Dr. Lajara, that on an occasion, about 8-10 years ago, came to Segovia to the Monastery of San Juan de la Cruz to teach some courses about Evangelism Explosion?" I said yes. Then he told me: "I have wished to meet you because you made the presentation of the Gospel to Desiderio, who was the priest in charge of that Monastery. He accepted Christ, and today he serves the Lord, planting churches in northern Spain with some Swedish missionaries."

Naturally I was interested in seeing again the parish priest Desiderio, now a missionary, serving the Lord together with other missionaries, planting churches in northern Spain. We had an encounter full of blessings, great memories, good food, renewing our encounter before the Lord and making future plans to start new churches.

Continuing with the development of Evangelism Explosion in the Iberian Peninsula, we entered Portugal where, by the mercy of God, we could also seek and train some key leaders, who were used by God to begin the development of the ministry in that place. For the beginnings of E.E. in Portugal, the first church that marked this beginning was the Church of God, where brother Rev. Antonio R. Pereira was the pastor in Amadora, Portugal. We had also begun the ministry in one of the leading churches in Lisbon, where Rev. Pessoa was the pastor and President of the Assemblies of God.

In one of the first clinics in Amadora, from October 25-30, 1985 we had 63 participants offering a wide variety for the development of the ministry in Portugal and even in Spain, because we had some brothers from the "motherland". Eventually, brother Pedro Pablo Reus finished his responsibilities as Regional Director for the Iberian Peninsula and brother Juan Diego Vallejos, of "La Biblia Abierta" Church in Barcelona, assumed the responsibilities.

Juan Diego helped brother Rev. Miguel Llagostera in the development of E.E. at the La Biblia Abierta Church in Selva del Mar, Barcelona. This was one of the first churches that began the ministry of Evangelism Explosion in Barcelona, Spain. They came to have a couple of clinics where they trained several pastors and leaders. Juan Diego was active in his church until he assumed the responsibility for the management of the Direction of Evangelism Explosion in Spain and Portugal.

The memories of Cecilio Lajara end here and the memories of his colleagues begin.

Chapter 4

Discovering evangelism explosion in Colombia

Dr. Pablo Méndez Nieto and Dra. Argelia Méndez

In 1982, Dr. Cecilio Lajara came to Bogotá to present us a ministry that has helped many churches in the United States to grow in an orderly way and that now was offering to help all pastors around the world.

At a meeting at the Bacata Hotel a group of pastors saw a movie that showed what had happened at the Coral Ridge Presbyterian Church in Fort Lauderdale. What impressed me the most was the multiplication of leaders involved in evangelism and discipleship of visitors and new members of the church.

As a missionary for Campus Crusade for Christ, I had been involved in evangelism and discipleship since my conversion. I had seen the spiritual birth and development of those involved in the student movement.

But within the local church, the scenario was different. Few people knew how to evangelize and less how to disciple. It was a job that only some trained pastors and leaders did. Almost all local churches of that time, 1982, stopped growing at the moment they reached 50 people.

In this context, it was a very attractive ministry that showed, as a result of its efforts, churches with thousands of members that multiplied continuously.

I was invited to participate in a Clinic

Some of those who participated in the first meeting were invited by the Presbyterian Church of Coral Ridge to attend a training for pastors held in January 1983. They had a name for this first meeting of pastoral training: Evangelism Clinic - First Level.

I was greatly impacted by several things I saw in that clinic and in that church: the quality of teachers, the passion and dedication of the local church evangelization teams, the quality and content of the materials, the home visits to those who were evangelized, and see how the ministry of evangelism in homes worked in practice.

Upon returning to Colombia, I set out to start the ministry in our church in Bogotá, following the manual I received in Fort Lauderdale.

The first students were my wife and three other people to whom I transferred what I learned. They were the first two evangelism teams of the Christian Community of Puente Largo in Bogotá.

At the end of our first semester of training in the local church we already had a group of 30 people involved in the ministry. Some as teachers, others as team members and others as new students and prayer partners. About 25 people had made the decision to accept Jesus Christ as their Lord and Savior. The ministry of Evangelism Explosion had formally begun in our church.

Each semester the ministry doubled and new believers were discipled weekly and were involved in church activities. It was necessary to recruit an administrator to be in charge of scheduling visits and obtaining materials for all participants.

Members of the evangelism teams continued receiving advanced level training and collaborated as visitation teams in the clinics.

First Clinics

One of the pastors of the Christian Community of Puente Largo found the resources for the materials and the scholarships for the clinics' participants. The first clinics were held in Colombia at El Encuentro Church and in our church, Christian Community of Puente Largo.

Then we helped to organize the first clinic of advanced level with teachers from Spain and Latin America. It was held at the Sochagota Hotel in Paipa, Boyacá with the participation of 200 people. It was a true celebration of evangelization.

I was personally involved in the ministry of evangelism at the Christian Community of Puente Largo from 1983 to 1995. I saw how this church became a "barracks" for training pastors. Every year evangelism clinics inspired and motivated other pastors to start the ministry of evangelization.

The Christian Community of Puente Largo experienced growth by expanding the base of leadership with the team members of evangelism. Other churches in Bogotá and Colombia also began to see the fruits of evangelism as a result of the training of members.

The National Board of Advisors was formed by the churches' leaders that were based in Colombia, under the legal entity of Evangelism Explosion. We set up an office and a secretary, and the printing of materials began for all the churches in Colombia and for five other Latin American countries.

The first clinics in Colombia were carried out by the Encuentro Church and by the Christian Community of Puente Largo, with the advice in the management of the clinic manual of Minet Malaret, the Latin American Vice President Secretary.

Pastor Oswaldo Casati of Argentina was the teacher of the first clinic of the Long Bridge Christian Community held at the Convention Center in Bogotá.

Missionary Support

Later, with the help of Roberto Searing, a missionary from the El Encuentro Church, Clinic Teachers were trained for Colombia. Other churches in Cali, Medellín, Barranquilla and Ibagué began to make first level clinics and the ministry spread throughout Colombia.

From then on, I was invited as a Teacher of Clinic in order to train in other national and international clinics, such as the Coral Way Baptist Church of Miami. God gave me the privilege of representing Colombia on the International Board of Evangelism Explosion for several years until the death of Dr. James Kennedy (its founder and president) in 2007.

I had the privilege to meet Dr. Kennedy and all vice presidents and other members of the E.E. Board of Directors, who enriched my life and motivated me to serve the Lord.

Thanks to the vision given by God to Dr. Kennedy, the ministry of Evangelism Explosion was established not only in Colombia but in 212 nations and 15 territories around the world.

That vision of equipping the saints for the work of the ministry included not only pastors but new believers who became trainers of soul winners for Christ. As the name implies, it was an "explosion" of soul winners.

Sunset

With the expansion of the ministry at national and international levels, there began to appear some inactive churches in the ministry of E.E. In the late twentieth century, we made a survey in all churches involved with E.E. and asked how we could improve. Respondents' recommendations included to reduce the program, making it more flexible, to simplify and redesign it with new information technologies.

As a result of the changes, "Hands to Work" emerged, which, more than a ministry, was a short and simple presentation of the gospel. What once was a vibrant ministry of evangelism, discipleship and church growth, turned into evangelism seminars taught by hired E.E. staff in each country. I remember the words of Dr. Kennedy when he met the proposal of "Hands to Work." He said: "That is very beautiful but it is not Evangelism Explosion." He was obviously referring to the missing of the multiplication of disciples.

Churches gradually left the program and few adopted the new materials. The Children's ministry called "Kids E.E." was the last thing remembered from that time.

With the passing of the years and the appearance of megachurches, the Colombian scenario also changed. Churches had grown, and being a Christian was popular now. Churches were filled with people who were looking for a "musical show" rather than an encounter with the

Savior.

Talking about training and visitation is now something unpopular. No one wants to train in personal evangelism. Everyone wants stage, microphone, lights, special effects, sound equipment, television and large screens. The topics of sermons no longer speak of holiness but of self-realization, achievement of personal goals, prosperity, leadership and politics. Today it is not common to meet a church dedicated to evangelization and personal discipleship.

But we know that the Church of the Lord shall have to return along the paths of discipleship and personal evangelization if we want to recover its strength and its multiplier character.

Chapter 5

Sunrise of evangelism explosion in Colombia (1982)

Rev. Robert Searing

The story begins with the trip of pastor George Hall with his wife Miriem, to Fort Lauderdale, Florida. They took fifteen days of vacation in March to escape from the cold weather of Buffalo, New York. While there, on the first Sunday they decided to visit the Coral Ridge Church, and after the service, pastor Hall had the opportunity to speak with Dr. Kennedy. In the talk Dr. Kennedy mentioned his book *Evangelism Explosion*, which he had just published.

Rev. Hall bought a copy of the book, and during the week, at night, he and his wife read it. It impacted them so much that the pastor decided to return the next Sunday and bought two more copies. When they came back to the church in Buffalo, they gave me one (Robert Searing) and the other to another elder of the church, with the comment: "Read it. If you think it will help us in church, we can learn the method along with our wives and use it in our church."

The result was amazing! The six of us began the studies chapter by chapter. Before finishing the book, my wife Margaret along with Miriem, visiting a lady of Italian descent, led her to the Lord's feet. She was the first result of Evangelism Explosion in our church. Within four months, Margaret and I trained about six young people from our youth group and an unusual growth began in our church. We discovered the value of this way of evangelizing. When we started using Evangelism Explosion in our church in Buffalo, we had an attendance of 25 people. When we left the church to return to work with the Christian and Missionary Alliance, the attendance was already reaching 400.

Today this church has an attendance of 1,500 and there are about 300 who have been trained in the Ministry of Evangelism Explosion.

In August 1982 Margaret and I returned to work with the Christian and Missionary Alliance as missionaries assigned in order to help with planting a new church in the city of Bogotá. Before leaving the United States, I had written to the office of Evangelism Explosion in Fort Lauderdale asking for a book in Spanish. I was notified that it was in the process of translation. Margaret and I were expecting anxiously the book in Spanish because we were sure it was going to be a great help in the new church we were planting, El Encuentro.

I shared with several Colombian pastors and missionaries how useful this training was. I talked about the training clinics that were taking place at the Coral Ridge Church in Fort Lauderdale and the results we had seen at our church in Buffalo, New York. For the Colombian pastors, the idea of training people from the church and visiting, appealed to them very much. They would no longer have to rely solely on evangelistic campaigns. Four of the Colombian pastors were very interested in reading Dr. Kennedy's book and receiving this training. Letters began to fly between Bogotá and Fort Lauderdale and we received the news that the book was now in Spanish. This news increased their desire to take the clinic. During those days, a letter from the Evangelism Explosion office arrived, telling us that they would be willing to cover the expenses of the evangelism clinic and the stay of the four, if they covered their own flight expenses. The four pastors soon presented their passports to get the visa from the American Embassy and told their families and their churches about this new opportunity to receive training in Evangelism Explosion. The four got the visas, bought the tickets to Miami, and traveled to receive the training. It was difficult for them because of their little knowledge of English, but they managed and did well in the clinic.

Upon the return of the four pastors to Bogotá, we had meetings and agreed to create a group to start working in our four churches: El Encuentro, newly planted with 50 believers, Puente Largo with 200, "Tabenáculo de Fe" with 250, and the church from the south of Bogotá with 100. We began to pray, asking God to first supply the need for Spanish materials, implying the need to produce materials in Colombia. We made a request to World Vision in order to print the materials, the book on *Evangelism*. God answered and World Vision gave us $23,000 to print *Evangelism Explosion* (by Dr. D. James Kennedy) and other follow-up materials.

We began making plans to conduct the first training clinic at the El Encuentro church in 1983. Dr. Woody Lajara, Vice President of Evangelism Explosion, offered to come and direct this first clinic in Colombia. We had to change the schedule format a little because of the limited amount of people already trained in visitation, but this was overcome with those already trained, leaving in the afternoon and in the evening, in order to be able to meet the three outings required by the clinic. We had 72 students including Colombian pastors from Bogotá, missionaries, and a few leaders from three churches who were participating in this effort. The result was so fruitful in this clinic that after this first clinic, pastors, missionaries and Colombian leaders were lining up to be part of the next clinic. More than one hundred people surrendered to Christ on the three afternoons and evenings of visitation.

The flame of evangelism was lit by the Spirit of God and in the next few years we saw this ministry grow and reach other cities in Colombia. Four churches in Bogotá - El Encuentro, Puente Largo, Filadelfia Church, and La Cruzada Cristiana were responsible for raising the flame of Evangelism Explosion. Other churches in other cities offered their locations and clinics were held in Ibagué, Tolima, Santa Marta, Cartagena, Barranquilla on the north coast, and the island of San Andrés in the Caribbean. Outside the country's boundaries Evangelism Explosion was planted in Quito and Guayaquil in Ecuador, and Caracas, Venezuela. Then, through pastors and missionaries from Colombia, it reached to Costa Rica, Peru and Bolivia.

Here are some stories when the Holy Spirit touched hearts and changed lives through E.E. Bogotá: When Margaret and I returned from the United States after a year of ministry, promoting missions in churches of the Christian and Missionary Alliance, we began the discipleship of a couple that had given their lives to the Lord Jesus Christ with us only a few days before our departure to the United States. He was the chief chemist of Coca Cola in Colombia and at that time, she was the Secretary of Public Health of the Colombian government. Both were from the high society of Bogotá and we started a Bible study in our house with them. Within a few weeks, we had the privilege of bringing another couple to the Lord's feet. He was an

51

economic advisor for the President of Colombia. The two couples asked to be trained in Evangelism Explosion. They became friends not only with us but with everyone at church. Within a year the two couples were working in Evangelism Explosion as leaders and teaching others in the ministry of Evangelism Explosion. This went on for about two years. One day Eduardo called us (the Coca Cola chemist) to let us know that he had been appointed to run the Coca Cola company in Asia and his office would be Hong Kong. Eduardo asked me if Evangelism Explosion was used there. I told him that I would find out if churches in Hong Kong used it and if they used it in Chinese or English.

A few days later I received news from a missionary friend in Hong Kong, saying that they were using E.E. in English. Then, Eduardo and Astrid asked me to review E.E. in English with them in order to be able to use it in Hong Kong. We spent two days of 12 hours each day reviewing the verses, illustrations, and the entire presentation in English. Eduardo left first, in order to know his work and everything related to Coca Cola, get an apartment, furniture, etc. Eduardo called Astrid the day after arriving and told her how brothers from an Alliance church had received him at the airport, arranged with the Coca Cola Manager who was waiting for him, took him to the hotel where he was going to stay for a few weeks, and that same night took him to make an E.E. visit. Eduardo said: "I arrived running." And everyone at the El Encuentro Church remember what he said in his farewell at the last service before going to Hong Kong. "Coca Cola pays my salary, but I go as a servant of Jesus Christ."

This story does not end there. Years later, at the meeting in Fort Lauderdale, in a celebration for having planted Evangelism Explosion teams in all nations, I carried the Colombian flag in the entrance procession. After the service ended, a young lady came to me and asked, "Are you Roberto Searing?" I said, "Yes." She immediately asked, "Are you the Robert Searing who led Eduardo and Astrid to know Christ?" I replied, "I am. Why are you asking me?" She replied, "Because I am one of your spiritual granddaughters. Eduardo and Astrid led me to meet Christ when I worked as their employee in their apartment in Hong Kong. Later when I returned to the Philippine Islands, I met a sailor of the United States Naval Force and we got married, and now we live here in Fort Lauderdale and we are part of this church. Not only this but in Manila there is a church called the Hong Kong Alliance Church, for the many housekeepers Astrid and Eduardo brought to know Christ in Hong Kong." Glory to God for his faithfulness in His service.

But the story does not end there. After Eduardo and Astrid were transferred to Mexico City by Coca Cola, they helped the Alliance plant other churches there. Later, Eduardo was appointed one of the Vice Presidents of Coca Cola and was transferred to Atlanta, Georgia. There Astrid founded an association to help single pregnant women to give birth instead of getting an abortion. Many of them met the Lord through this ministry.

Now, regarding the other couple who studied together with Eduardo and Astrid. As I said, Mario was an economic advisor for the President of Colombia. When the president changed, Mario and Estela returned to Pereira, where they were from, to work at the University of Pereira. They began attending the Cumberland Presbyterian Church, which was a few blocks from their home, and both began to help in that church. Mario was well known in the city for being the president's advisor, a teacher and part of a military family,

He began to share the gospel using Evangelism Explosion, but he realized that it was necessary to disciple these new believers before suggesting that they start going to an evangelical church. As their apartment had room for about 15 people, when they had 13 surrendered to Christ, he and Estela invited them to go to their home every week to be discipled in the Word of God. More than 20 years have passed, and Mario and Estelita still follow the same rhythm. Some years ago, I visited them in Pereira. I participated in the group of 13 they had at that moment. I was invited to preach at the Presbyterian Church where I had preached when I was a missionary in Colombia in the 1990s. What a difference! In 1996 there were about 200 people in the service. When I visited in 2008, I had to give the same message three times, each service crowded with people. The senior pastor, who was a good friend of mine for many years, joked, "It is your fault for what has happened. Most of these new believers are the product of what God has done through Mario and Estelita. And not only in our church; many of the city's evangelical churches have been affected by the work of this couple."

When Mario and Estelita arrived that day to church for the second service, he asked me: "Did you meet the person who was handing out the bulletins?" I replied: "No, he gave me a bulletin and continued giving bulletins at the door of the church." Mario said, "He is the Governor of the province of Quindío. A few months ago, he heard the gospel in one of our 13 groups." God continues working through the Spirit. To Him be the glory.

Something interesting happened in Bogotá. In 1993, an Evangelism Explosion team from our church El Encuentro visited the home of a widowed woman, a Jehovah's Witness, who had requested a visit after seeing the life changing of a neighbor. She gave her life to Christ and asked me to be her mentor in order to explain to her where the Witnesses had twisted the Word of God. I could help her better understand the Word of God and she joined the group of E.E. training.

Margaret and I left for a year in order to visit some churches in the United States and when we returned, one Sunday I met this widowed woman with a large group of her family. She introduced herself and during the talk with them, which lasted for a while, I discovered that all had been Jehovah's Witnesses, but she, with her knowledge of the Word of God, her training in E.E. and filled with the Holy Spirit, had been able to bring 21 members of her family from the Witnesses' error to the truth of Christ. E.E. works very well in the family in Latin America and we have seen that after seeing the change in the life of the first person who gives himself to Christ, soon it's seen that the whole family surrender to the Lord.

Perhaps the most impressive clinic for me was the one that took place in San Andrés and Providencia Islands. The team that would teach at the clinic arrived safely to the island, and it was formed by Dr. Woody Lajara, Rev. Ray Castro and his wife from California, the Baptist missionary who at that time lived on the island, and me (Roberto Searing). Pastor Stevens and others from the island took us to get to know the island a bit and visited the place they had rented for the clinic. Everything was in order. The first meeting was arranged for two in the afternoon. We had about 30 pastors and church leaders from the two islands.

At the moment we began and when we turned on the projector, we heard sounds like those of thunder, and the light went out. We did not know at that time what had happened but within a few minutes, we heard from people outside the place where we were gathered what had happened. It was a terrorist act against the President of Colombia, on the dock where a warship of the Colombian Naval Force was docked. In the attack they also destroyed the energy equipment that supplied the electricity for the entire island.

The classroom no longer had electric power to use the projector, nor for the air conditioner. In a short time, the classroom was hotter than outside, because the roof was made of metal. We decided to move on despite what had happened. We had daylight, but visits at night were going to be difficult because the island had few streets with names, there were only roads between coconut palms. Some of the Baptist Church people went to buy flashlights, batteries and candles to use at night. Only some hotels had their own power plants. One of the pastors said, "It seems that the devil does not want us to hold this clinic." But God, the Holy Spirit, is much more powerful than the devil and all his demons.

The training classes went on, learning how to present their testimonies. Pastors are the most difficult to teach because they always want to take longer than required. Learning verses and illustrations were much easier. For the practices, the trained ones took small groups outside, under the shade of the palm trees, with a little breeze, to practice presentations. Some of the coaches decided to make visits in the afternoon before it got dark. Others looked for children from the neighborhood to guide them, so that they could know which way to reach the families designated for visits. Pastor Castro's wife went with other women to the beaches and they shared the gospel there.

Each night, after supper, the teams would go out to make the scheduled visits. The reports presented every night after visits were very encouraging with good results.

A visit made by one of the teachers was very special. He and his team of two trainee pastors arrived at a house. The night was very dark and there was not a single candle, and the teacher had no flashlight. He asked for the person who had requested the visit and heard the answer in the dark, "Here I am listening." He began the presentation, asking questions and receiving answers from the man of the house. After making the entire presentation, he asked the question, "Do you want to accept Christ as your Savior and Lord of your life?" He heard the answer "Yes." And then he heard, "Me too, and me, me, me, me, me, me, me". Then the teacher asked, how many are here? The man of the house replied. "Me, my wife and our seven children."

On the last night, after finishing and reviewing all the decisions, we found that 253 people had made a profession of faith in Jesus Christ. The clinic had been blessed by God despite all the problems due to the lack of light and discomfort because of no air conditioning. A few months later, we received at the office in Bogotá a letter from the pastor of the Baptist Church of San Andrés, saying that the church had a baptism on a Sunday afternoon, baptizing about 170 people, most of them testified that they came to know Christ during the Evangelism Explosion clinic.

E.E. trainees in Colombia have shown great courage by going to places where foreign missionaries couldn't go, and in some cases, women leaders taught clinics where the FARC [Revolutionary Armed Forces of Colombia] and cocaine producers were. They held clinics in Muzo - a center of emerald mines, where no government control exists. Other teams went to Putumayo, where the FARC charged them a tax for staying in the town and using the airport, as soon as they got off the plane that had taken them to Puerto Asís, as if they were the government of that city. But they did not bother them at the clinic itself, which was carried out with a group of pastors and leaders from the region.

Something very special happened at the Cruzada Cristiana Church (south of Bogotá) that not only impacted many evangelical churches in Colombia, but has been a blessing in other parts of the world.

The Cruzada Cristiana Church took seriously its ministry to evangelize using E.E. They assigned a full-time pastor to take responsibility for the training and work of organizing the E.E., and making visits.

A man from a neighborhood far south of Bogotá (two hours by bus) who had given his life to the Lord asked to be trained in order to evangelize his neighborhood. He had a daughter Mónica in fourth grade at the church school. As her father came every Tuesday to first be trained and then as a teacher, his daughter waited for him at church

56

after school in order to return home together. It was a two-hour trip on bus from church to their house.

This girl was very bright and by listening to all the teachings her father received, she quickly learned the whole outline of the presentation, with memorized verses and illustrations - in other words, the whole presentation. But at that time, according to E.E. rules, only those over 18 could be trained, so she did not receive her E.E. diploma.

But Mónica, around 10 years old, as she had to travel on the same bus every day to go to school and back, began to ask the Lord for an opportunity to share the gospel with the people that traveled from her neighborhood to work in Bogotá. The Spirit of God gave her the idea of singing choruses and hymns of the church where she studied and attended Sunday school. The occupants of the bus enjoyed the songs and one day, after several weeks of singing on her trips, a passenger said, "Don't you know anything else than choruses? Which are very nice." Then she started to recite Bible verses that she had learned in Sunday school.

Finally one evening, returning from school, one person said, "Mónica, what are all these songs and verses you've recited?" She replied, "May I ask you a question?" The man replied, "Of course." Mónica asked, "If you were to die today, would you be sure to go to heaven?" The man replied, "No one can be sure of going to heaven." Other passengers on the bus said almost the same thing.

Then Mónica answered by saying, "Then I have for you the best news in this world. May I explain to you this truth?" Everyone on the bus was listening with interest. Mónica then made a complete exposition of the presentation of the gospel with every verse and illustration. She ended by asking the question, "Do you want to give your life to Jesus Christ and receive the gift of eternal life?"

The driver, who had been listening to the entire presentation, braked the bus abruptly and shouted, "I want to give my life to Jesus." And another 15 people on the bus said the same. Mónica then asked them to kneel on the bus and led them in a prayer of surrendering to Jesus Christ.

When she got off the bus, some asked, "Where can we go to learn more about the Word of God? Because here in our neighborhood there is no church." Mónica replied, "Well, every night after dinner, we take time to read the Bible and pray. I think my father would let you come to our house."

A few weeks later, on a Sunday, Mónica's father approached the pastor of the ministry of Evangelism Explosion. He asked him for help because every night up to 50 people were arriving at his house to participate in the reading of the Word of God and prayer. Today, there is a Cruzada Christian Church in that neighborhood, with its own building and an attendance on Sundays of more than 500 people. And all because a ten-year old girl shared the gospel in a bus returning home after school.

When this reached the ears of the Evangelism Explosion office in the United States, they asked a question, "How was it possible that a ten-year-old girl was trained?" Because it isn't allowed to train people under 18. The E.E. office sent the Vice President in order to verify what Mónica had done. The result was positive and we began the preparation of a special manual to prepare children to share the gospel using the E.E. presentation as basis. Colombia was the first country where we made the first manual to teach children so they could present the gospel.

Now E.E. for children is being used in many nations of the world. There is a missionary lady on the Islands of Indonesia who has already founded three churches, reaching first children in the streets of the city and then the parents who, hearing the gospel from their children, have given themselves to Christ.

Now I want to tell you about Libardo and Solangel Barrios, and the work of E.E. at El Encuentro Church in Bogotá, Colombia, what God the Holy Spirit did in them and for them.

One day Margaret and I received a phone call from a woman who was being trained in the ministry of Evangelism Explosion. She asked us to talk to a couple who were her friends. We accepted and agreed a day and time to visit them. The man of the house, Libardo, was someone with experience in accounting and managed several accounts of highly recognized companies in Colombia. He and his wife opened the door of their home and that night Libardo gave himself to Christ. His wife Solangel had already made the decision with the friend that asked for the visit. It began a friendship that continues to this day. Within a short time, they were baptized and became part of the Evangelism Explosion group that was being trained.

The two of them surrendered wholeheartedly to the ministry of E.E. After a year of participating, Libardo and his wife asked to be equipped as training teachers. They took all levels of study offered by E.E. (in Colombia we already had six levels to train people in the best possible way). The first thing Solangel and Libardo did was to bring their children to the knowledge of Christ and they all gave themselves to serve the Lord at El Encuentro Church in different ministries.

One day Libardo asked us for a fairly large amount of E.E. materials. He told me that he and his wife were going to take some "vacation days" in Melgar where they had a summer house, near the city of Girardot. Then he told me something that seemed a bit odd. He said he would visit the three evangelical churches in the city of Girardot and tell the pastors about the E.E. ministry. He didn't say anything else. About three months passed and my assistant at the E.E. office told me that Libardo had come three times during the last three months to get more material - Gospels of John, New Testaments, some Bibles, and over a thousand tracts of E.E. presentation.

One Sunday Libardo and Solangel arrived at El Encuentro Church with an incredible joy. They began telling everyone how special their "vacation" had been. On Monday, Libardo and Solangel appeared in the office and gave me the news of what God had done in those three months of "vacation."

Libardo gave me a list of over 700 people who had made a profession of faith in Jesus Christ. He also told me that the three pastors of the evangelical churches in Girardot were coming to Bogota in order to talk to us because they didn't have enough people ready to disciple so many new believers. Libardo introduced me to the idea of asking some of those E.E. trained members of our Church El Encuentro, go to Melgar and Girardot every week to teach about Christian life. When the pastors arrived, we had ready six teaching teams of three people on each team, and we could fulfill what we promised. The three churches hosted and fed the believers.

The ministry in the churchers of Girardot continued until the new believers were baptized in their churches. Not only that but also the three pastors were sent by their churches to participate and be trained in E.E. On one occasion when Margaret and I went to Melgar, Libardo took us in his car to see where the churches were located and showed us how the three churches had to expand their church building for growth. All this was done by a couple that took seriously the mandate of taking the gospel to their "Samaria".

When our time to retire came, I handed over the direction of Evangelism Explosion to Libardo Barrios. Brother Paul Méndez has been the President of the Board running E.E. for all these years since he was part of the first four who went to Miami, Florida to be trained in E.E.

ECUADOR

I must also write about what God did through E.E. in Ecuador. In 1985 my wife and I started teaching E.E. once a year in a clinic at El Batán Church, of the Christian and Missionary Alliance in Quito. Within a year we had to add the Assemblies of God Church in Guayaquil. Using these two churches, hundreds of pastors and leaders have been trained in E.E. The two in charge in Ecuador are now Mrs. Irma de Maya and Mr. Carlos Varela. He was also the one who accompanied my son Marcos Searing to carry out the first clinic in Chiclayo, Peru and the Church of the Christian and Missionary Alliance.

For several years, Margaret and I (with the blessing of the C&MA and its office in the United States and the Mission of the C&MA in Colombia) ministered in E.E. for three months every year in Ecuador. A humorous note: On one occasion, travelling down from Quito to Guayaquil, we ran into a car competition. Our car had Colombian plates, so at one point a traffic police directed us to a road we didn't know, thinking we were part of the competition. They had a food and gas station on the road for the contestants and there they discovered we were not part of the competition. After making us wait almost two hours for all the cars of the competition to pass, they let us continue our way. As it delayed us to reach Guayaquil for a planning with the E.E. directors in Guayaquil, I put my foot very hard on the gas pedal. I passed several cars of the competition, some stranded and others going slowly. When we arrived in Guayaquil a little late because of the competition problems, everyone at the meeting laughed at what happened. The rest of the time, while visiting churches in southern Ecuador, we were careful not to travel during competition days in that region of the country.

COSTA RICA

In 1985 God allowed us to carry out the first E.E. Clinic in Costa Rica. We had 21 Costa Rican pastors in the first clinic in the city of San José at the Assemblies of God Bible Institute. My son Marcos was studying Spanish with his wife at the Language School in San José and as both were trained in E.E. I could use their help in teaching. Since most of the pastors were from the city, I was able to take more time and give more emphasis on managing the outline presentation and add more visits at night in order to ensure each pastor had the opportunity to present the Gospel.

I finished my work at the end of 1999 in Colombia, handing over the direction of the work in Colombia to Mr. Libardo Barrios. Mark Searing, my son, was responsible for the work in Ecuador and a pastor of the Assemblies of God assumed the responsibility in Costa Rica.

Chapter 6

History and development of the ministry of Evangelism Explosion in Mexico (1981)

Eng. Nahúm and Cristina Vega

The Ministry of Evangelism Explosion in Mexico began in 1981 after some pastors and leaders of Mexico were invited by Dr. Cecilio Lajara, as Vice President of E.E. in Latin America, to take a clinic of Evangelism Explosion in the city of Fresno, California.

Personally speaking, this clinic was of great impact on my personal life. In one of the trainings that took place during the clinic, the coach of our team, Pastor Ray Castro, prayed before leaving the church and asked the Lord for a divine appointment. We arrived at a certain place in an area of the city of Fresno. He asked us to get out of the car and prayed again for a divine appointment. We passed some houses watching if there were people inside. Suddenly we saw a young man in his living room and Pastor Ray Castro knocked on the door. The young man came out and once we introduced ourselves, we asked to come into his house for a brief conversation. The young man agreed and we saw how our coach made a presentation of the Gospel, brief and concise according to the teaching we had received at the clinic. That young man accepted and received the gift of eternal life.

He was invited to participate in the youth group of the church, which he accepted and thanked us for the visit, because that very afternoon he had to decide if he was going to be involved in a criminal group. We witnessed when his phone rang and he replied to someone not to count on him, and it was definite. This was of great impact for me and the other leader who was also part of the team, as we clearly saw the Lord's answer to the prayer we had made before the visit. It was truly a divine appointment.

Once we returned to Mexico, at our church "Centro Cristiano Juan 14:6" in Guadalajara, Jalisco, we took on the task of implementing the ministry of E.E. for adults, according to the instructions received at the clinic in Fresno. After training and certifying 26 church members, we accepted the invitation from Dr. Cecilio Lajara to organize the first E.E. clinic for pastors and leaders in Mexico. This clinic was held in September 1983.

Forty-four pastors attended from different churches in Mexico, including a pastor from Costa Rica, a leader from Puerto Rico and a pastor from Ecuador. During this first Evangelism Explosion clinic in Mexico, with three days dedicated to practical training, the Gospel was presented to 184 people, and 97 received the gift of eternal life. After the clinic, the people who made a profession of faith continued with the discipleship program and were invited to church in order to take a special class for new believers.

In a year and a half, we saw church membership grow. After this experience the church officially implemented the ministry of Evangelism Explosion and also the commitment to offer a clinic every year and the opportunity for other churches to implement Evangelism Explosion in their churches, with the purpose of equipping all church members to fulfill the Great Commission.

Since 1984, Evangelism Explosion clinics were offered annually in the cities of Guadalajara, Monterrey, Villahermosa, and other cities were being added. This is how the ministry of Evangelism Explosion was implemented in the Mexican Republic through clinics that were taught every year, training pastors and church leaders of different denominations so that they could train all their members. But this was not only in Mexico, because God allowed us to support, through clinics, the ministry of Evangelism Explosion in other countries of Latin America including the United States in the Hispanic area.

There have been very special experiences where we have seen the hand of God helping and supporting the ministry of Evangelism Explosion in Mexico. The task has not been easy but the Lord has always been by our side. I remember very well one afternoon, when I received a call from Dr. Cecilio Lajara (as Vice President of Evangelism Explosion in Latin America) inviting me to be in charge of the E.E. ministry in Mexico as Regional Director. By that time, I had managed to combine my secular job with the church. The secular job I had for a few years was as an air traffic controller, first at the Mexico City airport and later at the airport in Guadalajara, Jalisco.

I asked Dr. Lajara to give me the opportunity to pray, discuss it with my family and my church. I promised to call him back and let him know my decision, because it was about serving the Lord full time. My family agreed to support me, but I had to discontinue my work at the local church because I had to be constantly traveling. I also quit my job at the airport. Finally, I let Dr. Lajara know about my decision of accepting the position of Regional Coordinator, asking the Lord to confirm this call.

It was in the city of Monterrey where I received the confirmation from the Lord during the church's prayer time, just before the Evangelism Explosion clinic that was about to begin in La Trinidad Methodist Church. When I informed the pastor of the church of my decision to work full time in Evangelism Explosion, I also informed the pastors and leaders who were participating in this clinic to pray for me. I got written words of support that, due to lack of space, I cannot mention them all; however, I would like to mention a few:

"Dear brother Nahum. Thank the Lord for our friendship and fellowship in the work of God. Continue forward without fainting, in heaven you will be surprised at what the Lord is doing with your life. Well ... maybe you can already see it. Look what he has done with us. Thank you very much for your help and love in Christ." Jorge Comesañas.

"Thank God for your blessing in these six days. Thank you, brother, for the big sacrifice you made to serve God full time. I can testify that God has a great reward, even here in this life for you and your family. I am encouraged because this clinic was much more than I expected, very well organized by you and the congregation of La Trinidad. May

God bless you, your family and provide everything you need. With much respect and love." Rev. Juan Marcos Funk

"Dear brother Nahúm. It gives me so much joy to get closer to you during these four last days and I sincerely want to thank God for your worthy life, as well as your wife's and children. I had a great desire that came to my heart, which made me come to this clinic, and while studying I'm convinced that God had really prepared it since eternity. For ten years I wished to have 'more time' to dedicate myself to the work of the Lord and many times I found tests for tomorrow, 'courses', 'work', 'study', etc. and I came to feel that these had lost their purpose. Many times I shared the Gospel without the results I expected. Sometimes I was frustrated; however, God since eternity had a big purpose for my life and allowed me to complete my specialty three months ago, being currently available for a full-time service in church as a pastor's wife. When I came to this clinic I did it with all my heart knowing that I would learn a lot to train my 'little sheep' who I want to evangelize, and it has truly been a refreshing blessing. God has not only equipped me, encouraged me, but tremendously ministered through you, brother Jorge Comesañas, and La Trinidad Church. Thanks to Him for your precious lives. I want to tell you that I will pray for you so that God will always support you, but remember that OUR WORK IN THE LORD IS NOT IN VANE. God bless you." Betty Rosas de Morán.

"Brother Nahúm. Congratulations because you've accepted the challenge that God has placed before you, and you've taken it. You can say to the Lord 'the work you gave me to do, I have done'. I thank you because you've given us the opportunity to be confident in this task of evangelizing, which is so neglected. It's not just about trust, it is conviction and above all quickness in order not to waste opportunities. This is great! Being able to evangelize in a single meeting and in a few minutes. Thank you for everything, may God continue using you with power." Erinna Flores de Cantú.

"Brother Nahúm, God bless you and protect you. Thank you for sharing your knowledge with me and for the words of encouragement you've said to me. I hope this great ministry and call, which comes from God, will go forward until the world believes. We have prayed for you and brother Jorge in our prayer group, and for the opposition that surely will come, but we've come forward in this clinic and we will continue moving forward. Brother Nahúm: Continue to win the prize for which God has called you in Christ Jesus. Press on toward the goal. I will pray for your life, your family and ministry. In the love of Christ." Lupita Ábrego

So, therefore, I promised the Lord to work full time at the ministry of Evangelism Explosion International. However, my coworkers and some brothers at church did not approve of this decision. However, I did it trusting the Almighty who has supported us and has always sustained us. The Lord has helped me to carry out this ministry, He was always with me to solve the problems, because God has always been by our side.

I remember I was invited by Rev. Jorge Comesañas (pastor of the First Baptist Church of Coral Park in Miami) to be a clinic teacher. There was a week left for the clinic and the teacher who was assigned, notified at the last minute that he couldn't attend. So, I was invited by the pastor of this church and took on the task of looking for a flight to be a day before the clinic date, but there was no place on flights to Miami in those days. Everything was full, so I was on a waiting list. While I was at the Mexico City Airport, I found a friend who worked at the company where I was supposed to travel. He knew I had worked at the Air Traffic Control Center. He spoke with the Captain of the flight and made all the arrangements for me to travel. In this way, the Lord Almighty God helped me to be on time at this Evangelism Explosion clinic in Miami.

I thank the Lord for allowing me to be in this clinic which was a very positive experience, because 73 people heard the Gospel during the practical training, of which 52 professed faith, receiving Christ as personal Savior. At the end of the clinic, one of the participating leaders wrote a poem. It was spontaneous and very interesting, and if the space allows it, we'll present it at the end of this chapter.

In 1993, Evangelism Explosion for Youth was implemented in Mexico. This ministry was well received among churches, and E.E. clinics were organized for young people. So, as well as the Ministry of E.E. for adults grew the Ministry of E.E. for young people, which spread rapidly in the churches of different states of the Mexican Republic. Many churches have implemented this Evangelism and Discipleship training with great results.

Personally, I found to be very good the strategy of personal evangelism among young people, mainly because adolescents can be included in the plan, as E.E. for young people begins at the age of 14. The strategy is very good because they visit their friends and the friends of their friends as a courtesy visit from church. In the conversation they present the Gospel and many have been won to Christ, and most important, they follow the same plan of discipleship as adults.

The first week for a new believer is the most critical, therefore immediate spiritual assistance is very important. Once they integrate with the youth group at church (as in the adult plan) prayer partners are assigned committing to pray and care for them for three months. At that time, young people affirm themselves as members of the church, just as adults do in the Evangelism Explosion Plan for adults which they practice according to the E.E. strategy, as taught in the textbook of Dr. James Kennedy, author and founder of the ministry of Evangelism Explosion International.

In 1997 the ministry of Evangelism Explosion in Mexico achieved 15 years offering clinics in churches of different states of the Mexican Republic. Some churches offer annually both Adult and Youth E.E. clinics. An example of this is the PIB Church in Satélite, Mexico, which since the beginning supported this ministry permanently and thus many other churches that simultaneously offered clinics. Also, during these 15 years, Seminars for clinic teachers were periodically offered.

The results of these 15 years are as follows: 50 clinics were held where 1,444 pastors and leaders participated. People who heard the Gospel during practical training clinics were 5,224 of which 3,601 made professions of faith. There were 576 churches involved in the ministry of E.E. of different denominations, including 25 clinic teachers, who supported us either with adult or youth clinics.

In 2003, the 20th Anniversary of Evangelism Explosion was celebrated in Mexico. God allowed us to continue the ministry of E.E. permanently and of good quality. As a country we are privileged to have been collaborators of this ministry and also in the United States (Hispanic area), and some Central American countries, including Belize, Puerto Rico and Cuba.

Yes, this celebration of the 20th Anniversary of E.E. in Mexico has been very special for us. We give thanks to God our Lord for supporting us. He has always told us: *"Do not fear, for I am with you ... I will strengthen you and help you, I will uphold you with my righteous right hand"* (Isaiah 41:10).

In the past 20 years the Lord has granted us to carry out 94 clinics in Mexico, training and equipping 2,503 pastors and leaders with the help of God and 25 clinic teachers. According to our statistics, the results are: 8,449 people heard the Gospel during the practical training, of which 5,767 received Jesus Christ as their Lord and Savior.

It is estimated that in Mexico more than 800 churches of different denominations have been represented in these 94 clinics and more than 10,000 lay people in their congregations have been equipped with the Personal Evangelism tool in order to testify as Lifestyle.

As a result of this work we have seen in many churches the increase in the number of members. Some churches have been able to expand their facilities, others have been able to establish two or more Sunday services, and other churches have established cells as a result of growth of its members. But the most important thing is that many people have received Christ as their personal Savior. We have also seen that many church members are not coaches, that is, they do not train other members but make evangelism and discipleship a way of life.

God has also allowed us to carry out workshops with Hands to Work, where church members learn to share the Gospel as a lifestyle using the five fingers of the hand. These workshops are held any day of the week, for eight hours, and theory and practice are also taught. The Lord will always give the opportunity to share the Gospel. We have an infinite number of testimonies and experiences that the Lord has given us, and it's impossible to mention all the testimonies because we do not have enough publishing capacity in this book; however, many have been divine appointments and I can mention one at least.

Finishing a Sunday service in which a pastor had kindly invited me to preach, I was about to end when I noticed a young man coming into the temple and sat in one of the empty places in the back of the auditorium. At the end of the service one of the ushers told me that a young man wanted to talk to me. I went to the back of the church but the young man had already left, so I went out to look for him. When he saw me, he asked desperately for help. First, I asked his name because his clothes were dirty and he looked very strange. I asked for his name, hoping in the Lord that his answer was not "legion." He answered Alfredo and asked me for help again. I said "Alfredo, I can't help but I know someone who can help you, his name is Jesus." I presented the Gospel with the E.E. strategy asking the Lord to touch his heart. I guided him to a brief prayer, he asked for forgiveness of sins and received Christ as his personal Savior. His face changed, as well as his desperate look, and I invited him to attend that church for his spiritual growth.

That was definitely a divine appointment. The next day in the afternoon, they were about to take me to the bus station to return to Guadalajara, when one of the pastor's assistants came in and told me that a young man wanted to talk to me. I went to talk to him and I was impressed, and said: "Alfredo, is it you?" He was totally different; his hair was combed and he had clean clothes. He came to say hi in order to thank me. I said we were going to thank the Lord Jesus for the change he'd done in his life. I introduced him to the pastor of the church and a while later I received an email from the pastor where he let me know that Alfredo was working and assisting in the cleaning and maintenance of the sanctuary. As this testimony, there are many members of many churches that have implemented the ministry of Evangelism Explosion.

Finally, the long-awaited strategy to work with kids came to Mexico, the E.E. ministry for Kids that involves boys and girls between the ages of 7 and 13. For this new ministry in Mexico, God made a very special call to my wife Cristina in order to get involved in this area. Here it is Cristina's report:

Evangelism Explosion for Kids begins with a call from God to assume the responsibility as Director of Kids' E.E. in Mexico. It came right at the first E.E. International Clinic in Spanish in 2002, which was developed in Miami, Florida.

In 2003 we were asked to hold the first Kids' E.E. Clinic for Latin America, in a four-day training with an attendance of 60 people from different churches of Mexico and one person from Costa Rica to bless their country.

Mexico worked with clinics in several states with great interest in the churches. In 2004 we had the 2nd clinic in Mexico City. People attended from Brownsville Texas, Spain and Peru, so these places began working with Kids' E.E. In the same year, we were invited to give a clinic in Guatemala, training churches from several countries of Central America. In the experience that God has given me in children's leadership training and seeing the results in kids, the strategy has the power of God and He manifested himself both in trainings and fulfilling the purposes He has for each attendant.

In 2005, I was interested in reading the book *The Prayer of Jabez* and made this prayer my own. A short time later, God gave me a vision for Latin America. I saw myself on the Atlantic Ocean on a rescue boat, seeing all Latin America and the Iberian Peninsula. The vision was beautiful, but there is no time to talk about it now.

In 2007, the Vice President of E.E. Latin America, Dr. Cecilio Lajara, appointed me as Director of E.E. kids of Latin America. In the same year, the Lord led me to teach an E.E. children's clinic in Lima, Peru to introduce the ministry in that country.

Since 2007, the Lord opened up the opportunity to travel, so more countries were trained and blessed to introduce E.E. Kids. I made a trip to Costa Rica where I gave a seminar for clinic teachers of E.E. Kids in order to prepare them. I traveled in 2008 to Quito, Ecuador to share a E.E. Kids' clinic and introduced the plan to the country and a seminar for teachers.

In August 2011, I traveled to Cuba with a religious visa to share an E.E. Kids' clinic for the provinces in that country. This training was very special because I saw the hand of God helping us to transport all the training material, and for the first time we went out of the church to share the Gospel, without any restrictions and with the fruit of more than 100 boys and girls won to Christ. Afterwards, there were sent to Cuba the files of "Esperanza Para Niños", so they could print them, because the permission to introduce the books through OneHope was denied and so far, the government has not allowed it.

But the year 2008 was key to God's vision globally. This year I was invited to teach an E.E. Kids' Clinic in Bogotá, Colombia. There were five countries represented: Colombia, Ecuador, Chile, Argentina and Venezuela. God manifested himself in a surprising and supernatural way during theory and practice. I received a message from the Lord, it was long and wonderful. The key points had to do with the work of E.E. Kids that was being done, and its future. I mention some below:

- Confirmation of my call.
- God likes us to do the work with love and passion.
- Don't worry about money, he was going to provide everything.
- There is a permanente party in heaven for EE Kids.
- Open doors in Latin America to go in and out.

In April 2009, came a "Global Project of E.E. Kids in alliance with OneHope" and the invitation to attend, on May 10, at a global conference in Wollongong, Australia, where all E.E. Kids Directors of the five continents were called. Initially, the invitation was for Mexico and Brazil. The person from Brazil would help me during the conference by translating into English.

I prayed to the Lord presenting my need for a Mexican translator. Finally, the Brazilian was unable to attend and the Vice President of E. E. in Latin America told me I could invite someone else. I could see God's answer, and invited a former student translator to accompany me. I began with the procedures, and despite the opposition (as it was at the time of the outbreak of influenza in Mexico), God gave me a miracle of getting the visa to Australia in 24 hours with the Embassy closed. God had already determined his divine plan and the instrument for Latin America.

We know that God knows the desire of our hearts, those of us who work in children's ministries, called by Him for his wonderful work, in addition to the love and burden we have for children. We know God is the owner of the gold and silver, and the Almighty, our Heavenly Father to whom we ask for everything, gives us more abundantly than what we ask and who has control of his redemptive work in the world.

God has a special love for children and executes a divine and wonderful plan that only He can do, to crystallize a great and wonderful work using Evangelism Explosion Kids, as God's effective and powerful tool for these times, and OneHope Ministry with the economic power. The alliance of two international ministries: OneHope and Evangelism Explosion Kids brings the strategy called "Hope for Kids" for the end times.

Three steps for the process of developing the EE and OneHope Alliance

1. First was the Global Conference of E.E. Kids in Wollongong, Australia, with the Directors of the five continents attending, along with the Board of Evangelism Explosion International and the OneHope International Board of Directors. The Directors of E.E. Kids worked to redesign the new books, based on what we had, according to OneHope conditions and guidelines, the Teacher's Book and Book of Activities as color magazines. The third book "Camino a la Esperanza" or Gospel book. The editor of OneHope, who was also present, developed it based on the strategy of E.E. Kids.

2. Second was the meeting in Fiji in August 2009, where the E.E. Directors of the 213 nations of the world were invited, in order to announce the "Hope for Kids Project", the three books in English and the alliance commitments between E.E. and OneHope.

3. Third was the Congress of Nations in Malaysia which took place in March 2010, where we formalized workshop goals, church scope and the number of Field Workers to concretize the "Global Hope for Kids Project."

We were given the three books in English and the commitment of translation into different languages. In 2010 the Spanish translation and review was made in Guadalajara, Mexico. In the same year, the printing of the three books was carried out by OneHope and the request for materials was made by countries according to the goals already established.

First stage of the EE Children Global Project

With regard to Latin America, God gave me the privilege of conducting the first workshops with a three-day agenda as well as coordinating the goals of workshops and materials of the different countries and starting to develop the plan for Latin America. The first workshops were in 2010 in Buenos Aires, Argentina. People from Uruguay participated as well as national leadership. The second workshop was in Santiago, Chile, very beautiful and with very good acceptance.

The third workshop was to train the E.E. Field Workers leadership from different countries to concrete the Hope for Kids Project (EPN in Spanish) for Latin America. The participating countries were: Costa Rica, Guatemala, Mexico, Nicaragua, Argentina, Dominican Republic, Chile, Colombia, El Salvador, Ecuador, Chile and Spain. After this workshop, the countries started the Hope for Kids workshops in their respective countries.

To the missing countries (such as Venezuela), I traveled in 2011 to give a workshop for representatives of 20 churches and another in Panama in order to project the plan in both countries. Hope For Kids is a global project: In the first stage of three years 2010-2012 to reach 20 million children with the Gospel in the world.

In order to achieve the goal, we needed to: Develop workshops in 1980 in China, India, Africa, Euro Asia, Europe, Latin America, USA and the Pacific. Train 19,800 churches. Each church would train 100 children, achieving 1,980,000 trained children. Each trained child, will share the gospel using the book Camino a la Esperanza to 10 children and almost 20 million children will receive the gift of eternal life. In this first stage financial support was provided for Field Workers and for the development of workshops by the Ministry of E.E.

Through OneHope each church receives free materials to train 60 or 100 children, and the provision of materials for all underdeveloped countries of the five continents. Each continent contributed to the goal, with the commitment of a follow-up by E.E. and OneHope to report to partners.

In the first stage of the project, God gave us the opportunity to develop supportive material for workshops such as: CDs and DVDs of interactive songs and videos with the presentation of the Gospel. We are in the process of finalizing a CD and DVD of the Muppets from the book Camino a la Esperanza.

It has been a great experience working with the Ministry of Hope for Kids. The workshops' results of Hope for Kids (H4K) in Mexico and Latin America are as follows:

66	Hope for Kids workshops
4,562	Participating Leaders
2,504	Participating churches
10,376	Children Heard the Gospel
8,028	Children made profesión of faith
822	Participating churches
11,401	Children trained to shre the Gospel, each of them Will share the Gospel with 10 children
114,010	Children Will hear the Gospel

It is amazing and impressive to see how a boy or girl of barely 8 or 9 years of age, once trained, is able to share the Gospel with another child with an object they call "treasure" and lead him/her to receive the gift of eternal life. And not only to another child. We heard the story of a girl who came home after an E.E. Kids' class with a peanut in her hand and her grandmother asked her what the peanut was for. The girl opened the peanut (that had previously been prepared), took out a small strip with some drawings and said: "Look grandma! Here it says that Jesus is God, that He came from heaven to earth, lived a perfect life, died on the cross, was buried but rose again and now he is in heaven giving you the gift of eternal life. Grandma, would you like to pray now and ask Jesus to forgive your sins and give you the gift of eternal life?" The grandmother with tears in her eyes said yes. "So, put your hands like this and repeat after me: 'Dear Jesus, forgive my sins and I receive you in my heart as my Lord and Savior. Amen." The grandmother, after repeating the prayer, hugged her granddaughter and the next Sunday, she attended church with her granddaughter and the whole family. There are many anecdotes but it's not possible to mention them all.

[Nahum continues with the story:]

Regarding the E.E. Adult and E.E. Youth Clinics in Mexico, we report below these clinics' results in the period from 1983 to 2012. 141 clinics were carried out. According to our statistics 5,531 pastors and leaders from different churches and denominations participated in all the states of the Mexican Republic. The gospel was presented to 16,166 people in practical trainings during these clinics, of whom 12,302 received Christ as their Savior. The percentage of receptivity to the

Gospel in Mexico was 76%.

Simultaneously with the work that was done in Mexico during these 30 years, God allowed us to support some countries of Central America such as Guatemala, El Salvador, including Belize, also countries such as Puerto Rico, Cuba and the United States (Hispanic area). The results are: 25 Evangelism Explosion Clinics for pastors and leaders and the number of participants in these clinics was 590 pastors and leaders. The gospel was presented to 1,994 people, of whom 1,203 received the gift of eternal life.

It has been a great experience for us to have participated as instructors and trainers in these clinics, inside and outside Mexico with a great satisfaction of having served, not an organization, but the Almighty God, Lord of Lords. We wish to express our gratitude, first of all to God but also, our gratitude to Evangelism Explosion International for allowing us to work and have been part of this beautiful international ministry.

Our thanks to the pastors and leaders who made possible the realization of clinics and workshops in their churches, to the churches that have been faithful in their support, both economic and of prayer in favor of the Ministry of Evangelism Explosion in Mexico. We also express our gratitude to the pastors and leaders who were part of the National Council of Advisors, to all the clinic and workshop teachers, field workers, local coaches and missionary coaches. Please receive all our love and appreciation in Christ Jesus. Our thanks to Dr. Cecilio Lajara, who as Vice President of E.E. in Latin America was able to lead the ministry. We always received support when we needed it the most.

We finish this review with the poem of Sister Betsaida Casanova at the end of the E.E. clinic in Miami - First Baptist Church of Coral Park. - May 1990.

> Dear borthers of mine, this is the last night
> That this clinic joins to close with a clasp
> Here we are Maria, Raul, Pedro, Rafael,
> Ondina, Aquiles and Olga, Jose and Daniel.
>
> Daniel Matos, Doug, Juanita, Betsaida, Alberto and Gerardo
> Without forgetting anyone, Gilberto and Fernando.
> We have all learned and without exception

This clinic has been a beautiful blessing.

I have been particularly very blessed,
The food was what I liked the most…it was the best
The banquet was excellent and how delicious was the lasagna
And we will not forget the soups made by Comesañas.

By the way, Jorge has sung us even tango
And spent the whole clinic peeling and eating mango.
Work as an ant, ready as a gendarme
We always saw, paying careful attention, our little sister Carmen

And if Carmen was an ant there is also a busy bee
Fast, loyal and efficient, who is our sister Nildita.
Irma and Luis are two punctual folks that work with fervor
And with their presence they radiate joy and love.

Everything has been beautiful, but we are missing someone,
And as everyone knows it is our brother Nahúm
And who has been Nahúm? He doesn't need a photo
He has been the trainer and pilot of our plane.

He's led us on a high flight to the highest heaven.
Because with each word he shows the Lord.
To all, thanks brothers, to those trainers
That with patience and love are winning souls.

To our God, thank you very much for this effective plan
This precious tool of Evangelism Explosion.
And now to end, our souls all together
Will you allow me, brother, to ask you two questions?

Chapter 7

Evangelism Explosion in Venezuela (1980)

Rev. Valentín Vale

The beginning.

It was the beginning of the 1980s. I was invited to a pastors meeting at the free church "Dios Admirable" in Las Mercedes urbanization in the great city of Caracas. Someone we didn't know before, Cecilio Lajara, gave us a talk about Evangelism Explosion. Both the man, and the topic of the talk, were virtually unknown to our pastoral environment at the time. I was pastor at the "Centro Evangelístico" in Caracas, on the main avenue of Puente Hierro.

By then, Venezuela had a population of about 18 million people. Caracas, the capital, a cosmopolitan city, with three million people, was looming on the height of success. The great mixture of races and creeds was remarkable. You could feel the European and North American influence. A representative democracy was practiced in the country, although highly centralized for decision making.

As regards religion, according to the Constitution, there was full freedom of worship; however, it is more fair to say that there was "tolerance" since the official religion was the Roman Catholic. This presupposed that any person born in Venezuelan territory was automatically placed within the scheme of the official church. "Sects" was the name the Catholic church called the evangelical organizations that worked in the country.

The estimated total of adult evangelical practitioners was between 700 and 800 thousand people. In the Caracas metropolitan area, the estimated quantity was about 60,000 to 80,000. As you can see, Venezuela was a virgin mission field, and Caracas required special attention.

Venezuelan writer Juan Liscano said: "We already know it, Latin America was not a colony, it was rather a political territorial extension of Spain, of an absolutist (Catholic) monarchy that wanted to stop the course of history when it turned to the Protestant Reformation, in the rejection of the pope's power, in the industrial revolution, in the agrarian division and in the parliamentary freedoms. Our Latin statism is the fruit of Spanish heritage, and independence did not change that sign of centralism, dependence, bureaucratization and paternalism, where everything depends on the State and everything belongs to it, where private initiative cannot grow, but in its protective and invasive shadow."

That poor concept, of being a second-class people, has been enthroned in some evangelical minds, to the point that we find the following practices in our churches: The only one who can pray for a sick person is the pastor (priest). He is the intermediary between God and the church. Or this one: people have to come to the temple to confess their sins and thus be saved. It is also said that the responsibility of evangelism and discipleship relies on the pastor and the church leadership. Moreover, "special" evangelism efforts are made during Holy Week, Christmas, or during "campaigns."

These practices have cut off the fluency of Christ's mandate of

GOING and MAKING disciples. The Bible teaches us that anyone born again in the gospel can pray for any sick person or need. Likewise, anyone can be saved when traveling in a taxi, under a tree or in a meadow, if someone presents the gospel to them. Of course, the temple is the meeting place to praise God together. I agree that evangelical campaigns are good; but there is no better work of evangelization than person to person.

An experiential matter

It was not long before I received a formal invitation to a "Clinic" of Evangelism Explosion in Rio Piedras, Puerto Rico. I was curious about being "interned" in a clinic. But I was excited with the idea to go shopping to the beautiful island of Puerto Rico with free airfare.

And so it was, in the summer of 1983, about twenty pastors from all over Latin America met in Puerto Rico. The facilities of the First Baptist Church of Río Piedras reverberated with the many different cultures of the continent. The main pastor, Rev. Félix Castro, and his assistant, Rev. José Calo Castro, gave us a warm welcome.

Goodbye to shopping, goodbye to tourism, welcome Holy Spirit to the living reality of the evangelizing ministry. God had prepared us extraordinary surprises that we never imagined.

First a methodology: Memorize the outline: (Grace, Man, God, Christ, Faith). Then a paradigm: What to do? How to do it, and when? Finally, the practice. Pastors with more than 20 years of experience going in threes, subject to the expert guidance in Evangelism Explosion by young men.

This is how you do it

It was a long and beautiful night. My team was integrated by another pastor and an elegant young woman from the host church, who led us. The orders were strict: She commanded the group of three. Do not use large Bibles, only New Testaments. Keep your mouth shut while she gave the message. A lot of prayer in silence.

Once in our leader's car, we knew we were going to the city airport. We were told that we'd go to a "divine appointment." In other words, to find someone, in any corner, under any circumstances. God would be our guide and instructor.

The airport's hallways in San Juan seemed the longest of the world to me. If what we looked for was thousands and thousands of people gathered in one place, that was the place. For me, the illogical of the moment was to walk and walk from one point to infinity. I wondered several times why such a pilgrimage. I remembered the instructions to be quiet. Endless minutes passed until I heard her voice:

- "Here, on the left."

We headed towards a secluded corner by one of the exit doors. There, lonely, crestfallen, a gentleman with gray hair spent his time sitting and isolated from the rest of the world. We went there.

- "Good evening! We are from the First Baptist Church of Río Piedras. We are doing a survey among the people who visit this place. May we ask you some short questions?"
- "Yes, It's ok."

I made notes in my mind. The lady had experience in what she was doing. It is not easy to walk up to a stranger to ask him: If you die today, would you go to heaven? And, if you die today and God asks you, why should I let you into heaven? What would you answer?

The gray-haired gentleman listened and answered what was in his heart. I have rarely seen eyes as absorbent as his. Occasionally a tear peeked out from his "windows" when I hear that she says:

- "Would you like to receive the gift of eternal life?"
- "First I want to tell you something." (Tears now came freely)
- "I'm waiting for my flight because I go back to New York. I am very hurt, and I
know God has sent you. I just buried my son. He died in a car accident. He had just
graduated as a physician. Yes, I want that God that you have presented to me."
I can testify that, at that moment, at least two people were transformed. The gentleman with the gray hair, and me.

A better paradigm

My goals changed, my heart changed, my way of pastoring changed. From that moment the horizon opened up for me and the church the Lord put in my hands.

It was a silent and fluid work. As soon as I arrived to Caracas, I asked the Lord to give me five people from the congregation to work with Evangelism Explosion. So it was. We met in my office to teach them and every Wednesday we went out to the streets to look for divine appointments.

At first the members of the church did not realize what was happening. After eight months of work, the gossip began. The pastor was criticized for having a select group around him, the others were second class. Thank God, He breaks every chain. We prayed and the matter changed. Now everyone wanted to go out to evangelize, and that's it! We explained to them that everyone would have the opportunity to do so, that it was a process and that God was in the matter.

After two years, the harvest was very large. Leaders had multiplied and church membership doubled. We leased the property that was next door, we tore down the walls and enlarged the auditorium. I could tell you many anecdotes of what happened then, but space does not allow it.

The explosion

On July 15, 1984, I was appointed President of Evangelism Explosion of Venezuela. I held that position until December 15, 1990. We established an office in the city and began the development of clinics throughout the country. All the churches collaborated extensively in this work and it was very productive. I must recognize the work of "Las Acacias" Church, with its pastor Samuel Olson. Santiago Montero, his assistant pastor, also helped us a lot. The independent churches, "Dios Admirable" and "Jezrel" were great collaborators. Likewise, the Coalition of Churches of Caracas that included "El Redentor" Presbyterian Church, the Mennonite Church, the Foursquare Church and the "Hermanos en Cristo" Church.

Fortunately, we were blessed to see in Caracas a true unity among the different evangelical denominations in the country. Pentecostals, Baptists, Presbyterians, Mennonites, Foursquares, Missionary Alliance, Independents, all joining forces to evangelize and disciple the Venezuelan population. The Evangelical Council of Venezuela, which brought together more than 50 church and service organizations, was very effective with its platform of unity for the people in general.

The unknown Cecilio Lajara is now one of my best friends. His family and mine are very close. I had the privilege of helping in the expansion of Evangelism Explosion by traveling with him to Madrid, El Escorial, Buenos Aires, Honduras and Puerto Rico.

Group of national Directors in a meeting in Colombia, 2005, to review together the results of Evangelism Explosion and make plans for the future.

Chapter 8

History of Evangelism Explosion in Guatemala

And EE adapted for ethnic groups

Rev. David Gómez

I used to participate in evangelism activities, preaching in evangelistic campaigns where I was invited. On one occasion I accepted an invitation to speak at a church anniversary. After the message I gave the invitation to receive Christ and ten people accepted and came forward to say the sinner's prayer. A year later I was invited again for the same reason, which I gladly accepted with the purpose of greeting the new believers. Upon arriving in the city and sitting down with the local pastor, we talked about the previous campaign, and I asked him about the new believers, to which he replied, "Which ones?" I reminded him that last year ten people accepted Christ. Then, he told me very coldly "Oh! they didn't come anymore."

I felt frustrated. In my mind was a question. What are we doing? There must be a better way to present the Gospel, I told myself. At "La Biblia Abierta" Church, where I belonged, I had the responsibility of the ministry of evangelization. It was a congregation of about 35 members. In my plans for a month of five Sundays, I presented evangelism classes in Sunday School. The first three were the introduction of a tool, and the fourth was to practice inside the building how to present the gospel with that tool.

The next Sunday we didn't have classes, because we went out to visit the neighborhood in pairs. I was left alone, so I decided to accompany a pair. When we knocked at the first door, a very cordial man came out and received us kindly. I started the talk, identifying myself and immediately presented the Gospel, and challenged him to accept Christ. He still politely, but with furrowed brow, asked, "And how do you know I have never accepted Christ?" I had seen an image at the entrance of his house and because of that, I began a religious discussion, which I won, or perhaps he let me win. I really believe that mine was a real "assault" with the gospel, and as a result I may never have a conversation with this neighbor again. I felt frustrated. There must be a better way to present the Gospel.

The arrival of Evangelism Explosion to the church

One Sunday morning in 1989, after church activities, I was referred to a missionary lady who was visiting us. She wanted to speak with the pastor or the head of the evangelism committee. Although I had not recovered from my frustrations, I was willing to listen. She knew how to get my attention, saying "I'm looking for help, I'm a missionary working in a distant village, although I'm back from my church in the United States, where I received evangelism training, but I received it in English and still do not dominate it in Spanish." "So, how can we help?" I asked. She said, "By allowing me to review what I've learned with some believers." "Well, I think I can help you," I said, to which she calmly replied, "Would you be willing to meet with me one day a week for about five months?" I immediately replied, "Yes, let's do that."

We met every Monday with two other young people for two hours. It was great! She asked E.E. International for permission to photocopy the materials and so we all had those resources. We practiced among ourselves and visited several homes, which gave me confidence in engaging talks without pressure on anything and without feeling any pressure. At the end of the five months, she brought us together with our families to thank us for the help received. It was a very pleasant meeting where we finished knowing each other. She mentioned her name again, Eleonore Norall de Beach, and her husband Edgar Beach, members of the Wycliff Bible Translators, translators of the Bible into Tectiteco, and with great interest in the people of Tectitán in order to share with them biblical truths.

After introducing ourselves and talking about her gratitude for the help, which she said I had given her, I replied that what I wanted now was to present my bill. She asked, "And what is your bill?" "To teach me E.E. as it is." "Do you want to be with me for another six months?" She asked. "Yes", I replied. Then the condition set by her was that I should have two more partners in training, in addition to the two partners in prayer. Commitment made! I recruited the pastor and an elder to be my training partners.

The experience changed my ministerial life

It was wonderful! I remember a neighboring family that we started to visit. The couple gave themselves to Christ. They had a two-year old girl. We gave them the discipleship proposed by E.E. As a result, they joined the church, were baptized and soon became our partners in prayer and then partners in training. They became deacons of the church. That let me know that what we had to do at our church ministry of evangelism was E.E. In the development of that ministry in our local church, a pastor from another denomination visited me and told me that he wanted to be trained in E.E. At that I told him he should come with us on Monday nights for 16 weeks. He agreed and we started training him. Then a leader of another church joined and then two more from another denomination. So, we had four denominations represented in our Monday meetings.

After that, one of the brothers expressed that E.E. was such a blessing to the participating churches, that we should create a ministry to bless other churches in the country. We did it, and so E.E. Guatemala was born. The Vice President for Latin America came and gave us credits and authorization to print and use the materials. Then I was sent with two more brothers to receive a clinic in Belize, where we learned many things about how to develop events. In this way, we carried out the first clinic at the "Mensaje de Vida" Church with the participation of 40 pastors and leaders.

The ministry grew quickly and a second clinic was held the same year. Because of the growth, it became necessary to have a National Director. The Board of Directors decided that this responsibility should be taken by Rev. David Gómez.

Evangelism Explosion for ethnic groups

After four years of E.E. we thought we should give special attention to the ethnic groups of the country, as we found that there were terms we needed to adapt in order to make them easier to communicate. Whenever we wanted to make the presentation, someone had to translate it from Spanish to the language of the person we were evangelizing.

On one occasion, while communicating the concept of "grace", the brothers translated it as "thank you." That made us consider the need to translate the material and have it printed. For this, we invited various Bible translator friends and some pastors of Mayan origin. We worked with all the material and the first essay emerged. We sent this material to the E.E. Vice President for Latin America with the purpose of informing what we were doing, and if there was any other work of this kind in another region, because we would like to exchange it in order to enrich it.

Meanwhile, there was a plan to celebrate at E.E. International for having reached the 211 existing nations at that time (in 1995), a celebration to which we were invited to a year earlier, and held a previous session in preparation. But at that meeting an idea arose under my proposal, that we had reached countries but not nations, clarifying that a nation is a social group with its own worldview, language, and its own culture, and that these groups could inhabit within the territories of the known countries. The participating staff knew how to understand and asked the ministry of E.E. Guatemala that when celebrating 35 years of E.E. International we would accept the invitation to participate in the celebration with the purpose of promoting E.E. Ethnies.

We prepared a special presentation with the help of the Christian Academy of Guatemala (CAG), a school for missionaries' children in Guatemala. The presentation had slides and an audio cassette narrating the presentation. We collected for that presentation, experiences and testimonies in the field of work, as a man who told us that Jesus had to be a very good man because all nations speak of Him, and they say good things. To the question of where he believed that Jesus would come, he said that from the other side of the mountain because there is where come those who speak of him. A woman said that she couldn't believe that if Jesus is God, then, how is it that he came to die for her, a great sinner? Another woman had said in her language, that it was the first time she heard a good Spirit (Christ) came and sacrificed for her, as all spirits who she knew demanded sacrifices.

We saw a man named Elías, who was jumping with joy and laughing so much. When we asked him the reason, he said that a few years ago there was a huge flood in his village that killed his two daughters. He had complained to God because of that, but his claim was, "God, you've taken away my two daughters; now I ask you to give me one thousand Garifunas who believe in you, for each one of them." Since then, he told us, "I've wanted to preach the gospel and I haven't been able to, because the first six have accepted and I'm missing one thousand nine hundred ninety-four."

All this was very well received and we were immediately asked to lead that ministry. There was a great demand of believers who asked us to go to their countries to carry out clinics we called: "E.E. Clinics for Ethnic Groups."

Upon returning from the celebration, the Guatemalan team took care of what we considered would be huge. So, we studied the material again with believers we were already training at churches of different villages, which we'd later visit. But now, we knew that we'd have to do it with many more villages. For that, we would need to do it with more than 20 languages in the country. Then we gathered several translators, linguists and believers from different groups that we had already trained in E.E.

We realized we needed to hold an E.E. Clinic Level 1, which we conducted in 1996 with the blessing of "La Biblia Abierta" Church in Colonia Valle Dorado (Ciudad San Cristobal, Guatemala). This clinic was attended by 40 participants from different Mayan villages of Guatemala and Mexico. We might mention languages such as Mam, Tectiteco, Quiché, Pokomchí, Jacalteco, Chuj; and from Mexico, there were Chol, and Tzozil. Then we stayed one more week with all of them at the host church, in order to study each concept. That is how a great job was done to adapt the E.E. material content which we called "E.E. Ethnics".

At the end of the week we were committed to put into practice what we learned, and continue with field research to know what can be improved. We also committed from E.E. to visit them at their local churches in order to know the community response to the presentation of the Gospel.

"Tejedores" (Weavers) – Witnesses of Christ

Before continuing, I wish to explain that "Weavers" is the name by which we decided to call the "Witness of Christ." The vision is that every believer in Christ becomes an effective witness within his own community. This is possible with our relatives in the most common conversations by launching Bible story comments, so that the other person presents questions or comments regarding the story. Then it would be like adding "threads" to a conversation, which then, with his questions or comments would be like returning the thread, and the witness re-launches it with his answers. In this way, the presentation of the Gospel will be "woven". Having made this explanation, I continue with the narration.

For five years we were working and doing field studies to find out how this new material worked, which actually became another ministry within E.E. After analyzing different towns, their culture, language and their way of learning, we developed what they already had for generations: ORALITY, so that we began to introduce a new tool in E.E.: the NARRATIVE. We have made a huge breakthrough with this tool that the coordinator of this new ministry within E.E. took it to Asia and other places where we receive constant testimonies of how useful it is in their communities and regions.

Consider briefly what do we say by Narrative: within the narrative we have people who communicate in an excellent manner through orality. Here we consider people who by necessity or preference learn and communicate more effectively through personal interaction using stories, proverbs, songs and other means of expressive communication.

In "Weavers" we recognize that each one has his own values for learning but at the same time we consider that what is useful to some is not to others. That is why the narrative is the key for many people to understand the message and how many come to believe and make decisions. Thus, we consider that "orality" is not simply a matter of speaking and hearing the gospel but an opportunity to integrate Bible Stories by interweaving them with the most common conversations of the community.

We also need to consider that people of oral cultures emphasize the truth through personal relationships, respect and honor, and to learn this they emphasize observation and imitation. That's why in Weavers we believe that in evangelism these elements are very valuable for those who want to evangelize. We encourage each Witness of Christ to see the person as a potential disciple even before the person decides to accept Christ. So, learning to tell stories can lead to the presentation of the Good News, so people make a decision for Christ with greater knowledge and awareness of that decision.

We have lived the most wonderful experiences in the ethnic cultures of our countries. We have trained believers of more than 40 linguistic groups in Mexico, Guatemala, Belize, Nicaragua, Costa Rica, Panama, Colombia, Ecuador, Peru, and in Asia and Africa, countries where we have seen brothers, with special conviction in their spiritual beliefs, want their communities to know the Good News. They have dedicated themselves to translate the materials to their languages, making digital audio recordings for the benefit of those who don't read in their communities, and whose mother tongue isn't Spanish.

They don't really understand the Message as we think they do, when we present it only in the official language, compared to when they hear it in the language of their heart.

Chapter 9

History of Evangelism Explosion in Spain

Juan Diego Vallejos

The trajectory of E.E. Spain cannot be understood without the figure of Dr. Woody Lajara. He is whom God has used to launch, monitor and mentor his leaders for over 30 years.

Starting E.E. was not something casual or improvised. It was something in the heart of Dr. Lajara that had been incubating for a while with a passion and love for Spain that brought as a result different trips and much prayer before the ministry in Spain was formally initiated in 1983, leaving as delegates the pastors: Wenceslao Calvo, Luciano Arévalo, Rodolfo Loyola, and as National Director Pedro Pablo Reus, all from Madrid. This last man would guide it successfully until 1989 when he is no longer the Director, and Spain faces a difficult time for ministry.

In the next few years, a series of events unfold, difficult to explain, and up to three national directors appeared simultaneously. Some were self-proclaimed and the other designated by E.E. Europe, but without knowledge of the National Board. There was a person that, during two years, developed a frenetic activity around the country, but in some cases at a high price, reducing the quality of materials and seminars. As an example, six-day seminars were done in a single day, sometimes without material, and most of the time without training. We need to highlight the consequences of lowering the level of excellence, when pastors and missionaries throughout Spain copied, appropriated and made their own versions of the E.E. material. It brought serious consequences that even today it is difficult to have a clear idea of who was trained correctly in E.E. and who wasn't.

After a long time, Dr. Woody Lajara returns to Spain in 1997 in order to revive the ministry of E.E. For more than six years E.E. was adrift without a responsible person and without a national office. Although we must not fail to thank pastors such as Luis Antonio de la Peña and Juan Blake (already deceased) who, in the respective premises of the ministries were responsible for saving the stock of materials that would serve a few churches that during those six years, to train Christians at their local churches.

During this time, the saying "where a captain doesn't rule, a sailor has no sway" is evident. Supposed directors, teachers without much training and plagiarists appeared who made their own version of the ministry. The few clinics held were unplanned, ignoring all quality advice. Therefore, in the next few years brothers and sisters appeared who had participated in one-day clinics, without practical training or material. This caused a deterioration in the image of excellence that the ministry Spain had enjoyed.

In this period of reconstruction of the ministry Dr. Woody Lajara, along with a team of trainers mainly from Puerto Rico and Miami, made a clinic in Madrid with the collaboration of local churches of Fuenlabrada, Aluche and Carabanchel. It was a total success, and the commitment of these churches generated a period of local trainings, almost like rediscovering the ministry, since the existing materials were old and outdated. That would change over time, as we will see below.

This first clinic also functioned as reference to carry out a series of E.E. events under the initiative of Dr. Lajara, such as a SEMAC (Seminar of Clinic Administration). In the church of Fuenlabrada, in February 1999, there were about ten participants, including pastor Miguel Llagostera and myself, Juan Diego Vallejos, who would have a more decisive implication in the development of the ministry. There were also presentations, ministerial visits in Madrid, Asturias, Barcelona and Andorra.

Let's stop at this point to detail the visit to Andorra. On this trip from Barcelona where Dr. Lajara, along with pastor Llagostera and

92

pastor Richi (who was our guide) visited a missionary pastor, Stephen Horning. By seeing the enthusiasm showed with the idea of implementing E.E. in Andorra, Dr. Lajara decided to invest in him, so that he could travel to Los Angeles, California in order to be trained in a high-level clinic, but we did not know about him until 20 years later.

Returning to SEMAC, it was carried out in Fuenlabrada, Dr. Lajara challenged pastor Llagostera to conduct a clinic for pastors in Barcelona at the end of the same year. It was a big challenge, since Barcelona did not have so many trainers to rescue and update from the previous period of E.E. Apparently there were no resources to bring others from another Spanish-speaking country. Then, he decided to give me a scholarship to participate in a clinic in Miami, at the International Center of Praise Church, where a clinic for young people would be held in a few months, which would serve as a reference of how a clinic should be done with excellence. In a few weeks we managed to collect the cost of the flight ticket in order to travel from Barcelona to Miami, which was the only thing that was not provided, so that I wouldn't miss the opportunity to be trained better.

Thus, in July 1999 I took advantage of my personal vacations to attend this clinic. I made good friends there with an experience that subsequently would help a lot in the development of E.E. in Spain. On my return to Barcelona the work was distributed into two main responsibilities, pastor Llagostera would be in charge of the promotion and I was in charge of everything else: Selecting those who would help in the area of food, materials, SEP, prayer, transparencies, music, lodging, transportation, trainers, etc.

The clinic date in Barcelona was set for the last week of October 1999, and this first clinic host was the "Biblia Abierta" Church, of Calle Selva de Mar where brother Llagostera was the pastor.

Dr. Lajara traveled to the Peninsula in order to be the main teacher of this clinic, passing first through Portugal where he'd also planned a similar event, but it had to be canceled due to lack of notice. Dr. Lajara came to Barcelona where at the beginning of the clinic there was an attendance of 20 pastors from different Pentecostal denominations.

Although there was much to improve in this first event, the result exceeded local expectations with 19 people who received the gift of eternal life and a starting point to begin working in the reconstruction of the ministry with the greatest possible excellence. In the words of Dr. Lajara it was possibly the best clinic that had been done in Europe in recent years.

Then, after such hard work, there was a time of evaluation and future projects. It was a long night of talks, prayer and challenges.

In Madrid, Jesús Robledo is the temporary Director, since he said that due to his work, he was unable to develop this ministry full time, so Dr. Lajara was determined that pastor Miguel Llagostera would be the new Director for Spain. But he needed to pastor his church and offered his help to push the ministry forward as far as possible, but not up front. In that same meeting, someone timidly suggested that I help in the province of Barcelona and here it is where something happens, which redirects everything that until then had been discussed. Mrs. Carmen Lajara, which many consider the soul and spiritual column of the Hispanic Ministry of E.E. and Dr. Lajara's wife, spoke to those who were gathered there and with the conviction that characterizes her said that it was clear that God wanted Juan Diego Vallejos as National Director, which after a short silence, nobody was against it.

From that moment, I would be considered the new E.E. Director for Spain and Portugal and with it the complicated task of rebuilding a ministry in both countries.

A first step was the necessary mentorship of Dr. Lajara that began in November 1999 with a time in Andorra, a small country in northern Catalonia where he gave me the guidelines to start working.

So with a set of photocopied manuals, two churches just beginning the ministry, no economic budget, but with great enthusiasm, the new period of E.E. Spain began and lasts until today.

Between 1999 and 2001, six clinics of Level 1 and two clinics of Level2 were held, the only training formats available until that moment, plus the consequent local training, which was extended to 16 churches, implementing 180 students and about 500 professions of faith. Although the results were good and the fruit that God was bringing was very motivating, it wasn't an easy road in its beginnings, because the doors of many churches (that didn't have a good memory of what happened before with E.E.) were closed again and again. But new churches and pastors, with new illusions, made a renewed, current and fruitful image of E.E. in Spain. So, with the help of God, a new map of the ministry was formed, clearly indicating that appealing to the former collaborators was a waste of time. For five years we did try to contact these brothers who in the past were very active in the ministry, but who clearly had no intention of collaborating again.

Continuing with the evolution and advancement of E.E. on the Peninsula, I can say that in 2002 we participated again, after many years, at the meeting of E.E. Directors in Europe. It was something very positive, where we met the Executive Vice President, Tom Stevens and the Vice President of Europe George Vercea (the first one already deceased and the second one is retired) and someone very significant, Ken Silva, who presented the beginning of what is now called "Share Your Faith" (S.Y.F.) or in Spanish "Manos a la Obra." There he handed us a copy in English, that when we returned on a trip to Portugal, with the Interim Director the material was translated into Portuguese and then from Portuguese to Spanish, upon arriving in Barcelona. This material, although simple, could be used as a tool to open hundreds of doors through the one-day seminars of "Share your Faith." And once the pastors and churches discovered E.E. they were awakened by the burden of learning more at the different E.E. trainings.

Subsequently, a formal translation was made into Spanish in Mexico which we used for a long time until E.E. made a standardized material of that said manual, and which is the one we use now.

In the coming years, until 2006, Dr. Lajara traveled tirelessly to Spain in order to teach in clinics and support the ministry. In these years the ministry grew and spread throughout the Peninsula, consolidating and having churches with periodic and constant training in each region of the country giving much good fruit of souls to the

Lord, as well as hundreds of trainers.

In that period of time, 2006–2010, an important economic crisis hit Spain (and many countries in Europe and the West) which, unfortunately, also affected the churches. Many members were unemployed and many left the country in search of new opportunities, leaving the church economies staggering. This was the cause for many pastors to want more than ever to train their people and recover membership, but were not able to pay for it. Thus the ministry of E.E was severely harmed, without churches doing workshops unless it was almost given away.

I must add that during this time Spain received an invasion of missionaries from Latin America (that sociological fact might be the subject for a thesis) and many of these missionaries brought with them E.E. material from their respective countries. They started to do their own training by photocopying material, disregarding the national office in Spain. So, to the economic crisis of the country is added the lack of ethics of many Latin missionaries disrespecting international policies in matters of E.E. materials. We deal with National Directors that need to work secularly because he is a missionary in his own country but does not receive external support, so he cannot maintain a formal office, or reproduce quality material. When he seeks to decentralize the responsibility of the ministry in the hands of regional pastors, this doesn't help much, because the pastors have their own responsibilities and E.E. is not a priority. Moreover, some took advantage to do business with the materials, but registrations went down even more.

Despite compromising the family economy, I was forced (more by sense of responsibility than anything else) to take charge of the ministry in order to refloat it again, and this time without the invaluable help of Dr. Lajara, due to his retirement as Vice President of Ibero-America.

Even so, in 2013, in an important and unprecedented event in Europe, a ceremony for the 30th Anniversary of E.E. was held in Spain. Vice President George Vercea and President John Sorensen were invited to this event in Barcelona. Thirty-two churches and more than 500 people attended. It was an expensive but very positive initiative in order to get E.E. going again. Within the activities of the 30th Anniversary, Dr. Lajara's flight ticket was paid in order to pay tribute to his career and work in Spain. It was probably the most important and emotional event, where 12 churches and 120 people attended.

From that moment on, new projects, clinics, trainings, and visits started. This time we counted on a very positive help, which was the donation of a significant amount of E.E. material for kids, which served us again to open doors in churches to implement E.E.

Chapter 10

History of Evangelism Explosion in the Southern Cone

Dr. Guillermo Di Giovanna (with Dr. Juan Calcagni)

Introductory note: Doctor Osvaldo Casati was writing this segment of the book, which is now in your hands, dear reader. His memory was formidable to remember the innumerable details he always retained and shared.

It happened that the Lord called him to His presence on Wednesday, July 11, 2018 and his notes were left on his computer. The week before he spent in bed, and told me on the phone that as soon as he could, he'd write again. Those days of July 2018 are painful for us because we lost a friend. We will share a note about Osvaldo's life, because we value and thank God for the gift that dear Osvaldo has meant for all of us:

"Early today a friend called. Juan Calcagni wept on the phone, and told me that another friend of ours has gone to the Heavenly Homeland. Dr. Osvaldo César Casati Aristegui went to be with the Lord. At 83 years of age, his tired heart stopped beating, after walking and walking through "Brown" America, from the early 1960's until the first decade of this century, tirelessly sharing the Word of God. He belonged to innovative teams that brought the best of modern communication in order to convey the gospel, with the best of pedagogy and practical theology, to teach it and the best of ethics of the Christian life to model, through SEAN, LOGOI, FLET, Evangelism Explosion, Christian Development, HAGGAI Institute. He was a promoter of radio and television communications during the

70s, and many more actions. In all these spaces he left his mark.

He was pastor for more than 50 years, with several denominations, always kind, cheerful, hardworking, and generous. He gave everything he had and knew to others, so that they would know Christ and experience and share Him. Hundreds of Christian workers who passed through Buenos Aires searched for him and found sincere friends in Osvaldo and Marta, his wife. "There is a friend who sticks closer than a brother," says the Bible, and Osvaldo's life confirms this proverb. He was one of the enthusiastic promoters of the Juan Knox Seminar, He was part of this project with all his heart and thought, an example worthy of imitating and remembering, a life that inspires to follow Christ.

Glory to God for Osvaldo's life! We pray for comfort and strength for his wife, children and grandchildren."

Thus ends this humble tribute to this honorable soldier of Jesus Christ.

Opportune time in God's design

The appropriate time of the arrival of E.E. to the Southern Cone opens in Chile, with a letter from pastor José Mardones to the Central Office in Fort Lauderdale, for the year 1982. That letter was delivered by Doctor D. James Kennedy to Doctor Cecilio Nicolás Lajara, Vice President for Latin America of E.E. It expresses the desire to receive training and accompany the development of E.E. in Chile. In response to this request, contacts were initiated and a plan to reach Chile was carried out. In the city of Temuco, Araucanía region, the first clinic and the first implementation were developed. The Evangelical Society Church of Chile, of German origin in Temuco, was the host. Lajara, Casati and Ray Castro went into action for this beginning. An area of living evangelical presence, where other denominations took advantage and pushed the use of E.E.

At that time the Christian and Missionary Alliance was training its missionaries throughout the continent. In that way, there were good coaches, teachers and constant developers in all churches of that denomination. They were very helpful in the surrounding countries too, as in Peru, Argentina, Ecuador, Colombia, etc.

So in this way, with a simple letter, a fire of passion was lit to make disciples in the subcontinent. In Chile, another pastor of German churches, Edy Jacob, who served in Santiago, became another engine that promoted E.E. in the city. And many brothers from other denominations joined the effort. We must mention brother Alfredo Cooper of the Anglican Church, who enthusiastically opened the channel so that the denomination could use it throughout the country. There were many clinics and a lot of implementation; it's a fruitful ministry to the present. Years later, sister Jovita Medel was a hardworking worker, a tireless traveler to the whole territory, so that the flame that the Lord had ignited with E.E. did not burn out, and with an admirable dedication to the call, she never stopped motivating and training pastors and leaders. Investing from her own money, she continued promoting the development of E.E. in Chile.

Dr. Ernesto Humeniuk lived that initial experience in Temuco and has told us the following of that moment of birth:

"That torrential rain foreshadowed another kind of rain: The blessings in so many lives surrendered to Christ for eternal salvation. The morning in Temuco demanded to wait until the doors of the boarding school of the Evangelical Society of Chile at "Calle Alemania" opened, so I took shelter under a roof until dawn. I had left from Mendoza and was captivated to go down the snail roads of Portillo, and later take a bus that would take me to an unforgettable experience in the beautiful city of southern Chile.

The Evangelism Explosion Clinic, organized by "Pepe" Mardones, was the most important. There were distinguished exponents of Christian leadership, except for me, who was just a boy in a "poncho" due to the severe cold. There was no one to direct the songs, so I improvised as a master of ceremonies. The materials had not arrived, so barely legible photocopies were distributed. Dr. Lajara, the teacher, had an urgent surgical intervention for appendicitis. He was at a maternity hospital, but even there he "gave birth" to a nurse who received the gift of eternal life after the operation. Meanwhile, brother Ray Castro tried in his "bad Spanish" to teach us the material, without fully understanding what he said. It was the first clinic Ray taught in Spanish. I met there men like Osvaldo Casati, Edy Jacob, Alfredo Cooper and others.

Returning to Mendoza was full of joy. My first disciples were my wife Gloria, sister Maria Esther de Garay and the brothers Juan "Yeye" Molina and Bienvenido Torres. The church was blessed with dozens and dozens of conversions. Glory to God! Soon, we had a clinic in Godoy Cruz, that was the inspiration and multiplication of personal evangelists. Regarding this event, I remember that when I entered the International Baptist Theological Seminary in 1974, I met who was the guard of the men's pavilion, Juan Manuel Monzón, with whom I made some friendship. We always prayed for the conversion of his parents. When Juan Manuel got married, I took his place in the church of Villa Madero during the summer to practice my ministerial work. With time and since he graduated long before me, I lost track of him. When we were organizing the E.E. clinic in Mendoza, I received a registration from Juan Manuel Monzón, Bishop of the Methodist Church of Paraguay. I assumed it was another Monzón, not the one I had met at the Baptist Seminary. It was my surprise that he was the first one who came to the appointment. He explained that his wife was Paraguayan and that he was now serving in that neighboring country. After the end of the clinic, he wrote me telling that on the trip between Mendoza and Córdoba, his seatmate had received Christ, who, upon arriving in Córdoba, his hometown, his parents received the gift of eternal life. Glory to God! Prayers answered. On the trip from Córdoba to Resistencia, Chaco, another seat mate made a profession of faith and on his trip from Resistencia to Asunción another victory: five decisions for the Lord! Juan Manuel could not believe it. Sometime later, we traveled with Osvaldo Casati to Asunción to teach a clinic and we witnessed that the denomination that was about to close in Paraguay, the Free Methodists, was now a thriving and growing church.

We went to several places with Osvaldo Casati to teach together. But there was an interesting situation; every August we ministered at the "Encuentro con Cristo" Church, in front of Plaza Egaña, Santiago. One morning we slept in due to fatigue. When I woke up, I urged Osvaldo to get up, but we noticed there was no electricity in the house. So, we showered and prepared for the day's work. After a while we asked the host sister what had happened. She looked at us strangely, "What? You didn't know? Last night we met with our family to pray in the bathroom. We had a tsunami. Look out the window and see the damage!" What a shame! Not even a tsunami could wake us! We felt exhausted into bed after so much activity with the clinic that day. But it was there that we saw the blessing of a church in Ñuñoa growing and full of life. On one of the trips, pastor Edy invited us to accompany him to the bank, because the church was acquiring a cinema in front of the Plaza Puente Alto, and there we went to open those doors and pray dedicating that place that would no longer show films of low morals. Now the gospel would be preached! After that I had E.E. clinics in each church that the Lord allowed me to pastor: "Distrito Sur del Rosario," First Baptist Church of Bahía Blanca.

I thank God for the day brother Woody Lajara brought this blessed tool to the Southern Cone. Over time I helped to produce audiovisual materials, translate materials, and being part of the International Board. It is something that should not cease, until we have completed the task of spreading the precious seed of the Word of God throughout the world, until the King returns."

In memory of Osvaldo César Casati Aristegui

Ernesto Humeniuk.

On the other side of the Andes, there was the challenge of Argentina. Lajara traveled in search of old friends who had accompanied him in other previous ministerial challenges, and he found them. He found, as expected, Osvaldo Casati. They were like David and Jonathan; inseparable, and extremely hardworking. They added a referent who was unique in qualities, brother Jarczac, a businessman who served the Lord with dedication and zeal. And Lajara found Juan Calcagni, thanks to the recommendation of Casati and other leaders. Juan was a reference of the evangelical work. A national Baptist leader, but widely known, since his youth as a youth mobilizer, and then as an evangelist who collaborated with various ministries such as the Luis Palau Association. He was also a pastor of a church in Lanús, a populous city in Gran Buenos Aires, which is called "Lanús de Cristo," which would be a wonderful clinic base in the future. That church came to develop other churches and grow from 120 to 700 members. One of them, led by Pastor Alfonso Cubilla, was a clinic base and a great blessing to the ministry of the Southern Cone, after the 1990s. It also reached 700 members by 2007.

Dr. Juan Calcagni reviews his experience with E.E.:

"The 80s began when a dear friend, pastor and theology professor Roberto Jarczac, called to tell me that he was going to visit me bringing a brother who wanted to meet me and our church. I found the situation somewhat strange. I was just beginning my work as a pastor, after much prayer and difficulties to overcome in order to make that decision, and now I was going to receive a very special visit from the USA.

He came accompanied by another dear friend, pastor Osvaldo Casati the day we had agreed on. The visitor was Dr. Cecilio Lajara, Vice President of E.E. for Latin America and Spain. I was impressed by his seriousness and commitment to the ministry he represented and which had brought him to our church in Lanús, Province of Buenos Aires, Argentina. I was also impressed by the amount of questions and the thorough visit to the church facilities.

I must confess I was wondering: who is this Doctor who comes to our quiet church in our humble neighborhood? Why do I have to answer so many questions? Jarczac and Casati listened in silence, gesturing me to wait patiently. At the end of the interview, Dr. Lajara expressed his gratitude for having received him. We prayed and he graciously left with my friends and co-ministers Jarczac and Casati.

Several months went by and I received a call from my friends already mentioned for a new interview with Dr. Lajara, inviting me with my wife this time to share a pleasant table at the Sheraton Hotel. I convinced my wife that we could take advantage of being in that luxurious hotel, even if it was only for lunch. I must also confess our ugly custom that some Christians have to criticize, because I didn't approve of using the Lord's money to stay in a hotel in that category, but of course I did not say a word. My wife went with me, but told me to be careful what they proposed.

After the protocol greetings the first thing Dr. Lajara told me is that we might think he was using the Lord's money badly using that expensive place. I thought he was reading my mind. It happens, said brother Lajara, that the manager of this hotel chain met Jesus through E.E. testimony, therefore he offers us to stay for free in these hotels. In other words, it is cheaper than staying in a low-class hotel. I was speechless ...

The reason for the interview was to invite me to participate in an E.E. clinic in Puerto Rico with all expenses paid, travel, lodging, food, materials, etc. Immediately my wife whispered to me, what will they ask in return? They gave us time to pray and think. In a few days we both came to the conviction that it was a gift from God to help me in pastoral ministry and that we should not miss the opportunity. Needless to say, not only Dr. Lajara, "Woody", but Carmen his dear wife, today are our beloved friends. We don't know how much we owe the Lord for sending him to Lanús, and Woody for giving us an extraordinary help.

It is important to mention at this point of my story that my pastor, E. David Gilles, a great man of God, left this world unexpectedly by a stroke in June 1978 and as I was a close assistant, the church asked me to take over. I worked in a bank and wasn't in a position to leave that job. We were raising our three children, their studies and paying for the house we had bought. Therefore, I accepted the challenge and proposed to the congregation of 150 members that I would accept it with the condition that all of us would be involved in the ministry of the church. They agreed and with the impact of the pastor that the Lord took to heaven, who was preaching on the letter to the Ephesians, I asked the Lord for a message for the church. I prepared myself under that impulse and on Sunday I preached a Word that God prospered on the responsibility of each member of the body of Christ: The Ministry of every Believer. I made an altar call and all the church came forward, brothers hugging each other and crying. I was scared and said to myself: what do I do now with so many consecrated people? Instead of being glad I felt a tremendous burden. What to do?

It was a few days after this experience that the invitation came for the interview at the Hotel that I mentioned, with Dr. Lajara. I traveled with great expectation to the E.E. Clinic at the First Baptist Church of Carolina in San Juan, Puerto Rico. At the airport I received a very warm welcome. They took me to the place where I would be staying, the home of a church couple who filled me with affection and care. The clinic began and they sat me next to the pastor of the church. I asked him what he was doing there as pastor of a congregation of thousands of members. He replied that he wanted to have another tool for further growth. We were a group of close to 50 pastors and leaders from different countries learning how to improve our sharing of the Gospel. The clinic was full of wonderful moments and a teaching of great quality and value for the future of all attendees, and especially for me who was perhaps the one who needed it the most. I am extremely grateful to the Lord, to my friends Jarczac and Casati for choosing me to be interviewed by Dr. Lajara and then being chosen from around 20 churches he visited at that time. His decision was due to the fact that our pastor, before leaving, made us work in Evangelistic Homes, about 20 were working at that time. Lajara thought that we could use those Homes not only to evangelize but also to disciple those who would accept the Gift of Eternal Life when E.E. would be organized in our church.

The Lord, seeing my need to have a church committed to work and not knowing what to do, gave me this wonderful tool that is E.E., which gave us great results reaching in a few years from 150 to 500 members and in a few more years, to 700. After a division where about 300 believers left to plant two new churches, we restarted and reached 800 members, the mother church and 4 missionary locations in the same city. All this growth was due to working with E.E. teams and discipleship in the homes, as the Lord commanded us in the Great Commission."

To continue with the development of Argentina, it is worth mentioning that with the help of the missionary team of the Christian and Missionary Alliance, the first clinics were launched. At the Buenos Aires Bible Institute on Pampa Street, workers, pastors, and leaders were trained who would continue the chain, taking the training to the interior of the country. And in the big cities of the country, the ministry is strategically being implemented in: Rosario, Córdoba, Mendoza, Salta, etc.

In all the cities there were receptive pastors, ready to incorporate this important tool into their local churches. It was 1983 and the country was experiencing a return to democracy after a violent situation of military government and a war against Great Britain. The people were hungry to find peace and meaning, and in that context E.E. came to be a resource sent by God to local churches and denominations in the extension of the gospel through preaching and making disciples in a relational way. His values were very clear and direct: **_Friendship - Evangelism - Discipleship - Healthy Growth._**

A national office was opened at the Bible Society building, on 150 Tucumán Street in downtown Buenos Aires. Casati made the arrangements and traveled constantly to dictate clinics, and encourage implementations. I remember him often mentioning how he held seven clinics one after the other in different cities. Then he would return to the office, answer calls, receive pastors, print materials, correct editions... a tireless giant giving the best of himself to the Lord and the work of the Lord. Simultaneously he collaborated with Dr. Lajara in all the work of the continent, as his right hand in the Spanish-speaking countries that were adopting the use of E.E.

An experience of commitment to the present is the testimony of pastor Alfonso Cubilla.

"In 1983, my pastor, Juan Calcagni was invited to participate in an Evangelism Explosion Clinic in Puerto Rico, returning extremely thrilled with this tool which, shortly thereafter, he implemented at our church "Lanús de Cristo" Baptist Church, Province of Buenos Aires, Argentina.

In 1984, Pastor Juan Calcagni begins the first stage of Evangelism Explosion Level I, where I had the privilege of being one of those called to take the course. That experience completely changed my life, because at that time, I was relatively new as a believer. I had come to church looking for a perfect society, tired of the mediocre life I had.

I was a musician and my life included everything that goes with being a musician: alcohol, cigarettes, bad sleeping habits, bad eating, neglecting my family, etc. Soon I discovered that the perfect society I was looking for did not exist, and *that produced in me a crisis and doubts, without knowing exactly what to do. At that time, I discovered John 15:16 and understood that God had called me, not to look at the defects of others, but to bear fruit.*

It was then that E.E. appeared in my life and I fell deeply in love with this evangelistic tool until today, because I still use it and bring souls to the feet of Christ.

My pastor honors me by putting me in charge of the Ministry of Evangelism, so a time of work and growth begins.

Between the 80s and 90s, 13 Clinics and 14 stages of level 1 were held in our church, where we prepared 293 trainers, in addition to an undetermined number of people belonging to churches of the interior of our country, and from other countries.

Living these experiences was to live an immense satisfaction as part of this movement of the Holy Spirit through this tool.

On the other hand, I want to emphasize that another great man of the gospel appears in my life, he had a passionate heart for the lost: Pastor Osvaldo Casati. I learned a lot at his side. He trusted me and began taking me with him to have clinics, practically covering not only a great part of our country, but also other countries such as Uruguay, Paraguay and Chile.

I was in Paraguay for four years in charge of the Ministry of E.E. promoting and holding clinics of different levels: 1, 2, 3 and 4, and for Clinic teachers.

At the end of the 90s, my pastor honored me by ordaining me as pastor and putting me in charge of a Missionary Work, which is currently a beautiful church. In this new place we have carried out five clinics of level 1 and to this day we continue preparing soul winners and winning souls for the glory of God.

God has blessed me greatly in all areas of my life, but E.E. was the greatest thing that happened to me. It helped me to fulfill God's purpose for my life and the greatest satisfaction that means seeing the birth of a spiritual baby. It's the same feeling you have when you see a biological child born, a feeling that cannot be explained. I thank God for having known this tool and the people who trusted me: Juan Calcagni and Osvaldo Casati. It would be unfair if I do not name another great man, Woody Lajara, who in his heart was always to win his "brown" America to Christ."

List of Implementation Stages of EE. Level I carried out at "Cristo" Baptist Church, City of Lanús, with its members.

No.	Number of Students	Dates
1	4	1984
2	10	01/08/1985
3	24	01/08/1986
4	49	03/04/1987
5	29	19/03/1988
6	17	06/08/1988
7	20	17/03/1989
8	16	11/03/1990
9	26	15/03/1991
10	29	07/03/1992
11	30	05/03/1993
12	13	13/03/1994
13	12	15/03/1995
14	14	14/03/1996
15	14	16/03/1996
16	18	12/03/1997
Total	321	

At Lajara's invitation I participated with him in CLINICS AT THE "CRISTO" BAPTIST CHURCH in LANÚS:

- 9 Clinics – Level I
- 5 Clinics – Level II
- 3 Clinics – Level III
- 1 Clinic – Youth Level

CLINIC TEACHERS IN ARGENTINA: I have 20 in my records
ADVANCED SEMINAR IN ARGENTINA: from October 20 to 24 1987 we did one in Mar del Plata, with the presence of Dr. James Kennedy, Pastor Samuel Olson from Venezuela and Dr. Wilfredo Estrada Adorno participating as teachers. That was the Second Advanced Seminar.

At Lajara's invitation I participated with him in an E.E. Clinic in PAIPA, COLOMBIA, accompanied by Pastor RODOLFO LOYOLA, poet and Cuban writer, now living in Spain. Also, by the grace of the Lord and by the invitation of Lajara I participated in MADRID, SPAIN in a clinic with a great number of pastors and leaders.

Also, in May 1987, we participated at the INTERNATIONAL CONFERENCE OF E.E. LEADERS in Fort Lauderdale with Osvaldo Casati, Roberto Jarczak and Ernesto Humeniuk with the presence of about 2,000 participants and the representation of countries around the world where the E.E. Ministry had gone. There was a very impressive moment during the main meeting where, among other participations, there was a parade of flags from all the countries represented. By Casati's decision I was privileged to carry the Argentine flag instructing me to invite the representative of England to march together. I did it that way, and the British brother was very happy and willing to do so. It was a tremendous moment, where everyone applauded standing by the two flags that went together, because both countries were at war. We gave Glory to the Lord, because He made it possible.

I should mention other very active leaders: brother Rubén Calabretta was an active pastor among the Plymouth Brethren (Hermanos Libres) and other denominations to sow and develop E.E. in a unique and practical way, as is his style. His father-in-law, José Bongarrá, a pioneer leader in many areas, saw the wonderful opportunity that a tool like E.E. meant. He wanted to train all his leaders, but Rubén led him to the right path, the progression taught in the clinics, and that way he had huge results.

Alberto Ainscough and his wife Rosa, both doctors, pastors and active leaders at the Church of the Nazarene, applied and multiplied E.E. throughout the territory of that denomination.

His church was awarded as Clinic Base Church in 2007 with a continuity for 30 years of development in the country. They founded that church in Villa Ballester, in the Greater Buenos Aires, where E.E. was a tool of growth. In addition, there were planters of many other local churches. To mention as an example, in January 2005 we went to Bragado, on the National Route 5, where they had a developing church and a school of evangelism. We held an E.E. clinic for adults and went out to do our practices in other cities such as "9 de Julio", where they had people to reach and who, at the outputs of practical training, received the gift of eternal life.

The Assemblies of God church "Cristo la Solución," in the crowded neighborhood of Flores, Buenos Aires city, adopted the ministry and appointed a pastor dedicated to train members with E.E; and brother Cisneros, who did a formidable work, while the church grew locally he was planting churches in other locations in Greater Buenos Aires. They experienced exponential growth.

The movement "Visión de Futuro" [Vision of the Future], which Rev. Omar Cabrera presided over and developed, adopted E.E. He trained all his leaders at the "Rafaela" Seminary and in local churches in large cities of the country, with immense numerical growth, within a Neopentecostal type structure.

Many years later, in 2009 we went to Córdoba in order to motivate a church that had had a great growth with E.E., the Baptist church of Patricios neighborhood. The main pastor, Leopoldo Benedetto, received me at his home. We evaluated the past with E.E. and saw the possibility of resuming its use there. Then, he began to evaluate the availability of human resources, based on the active leaders trained in previous years. And suddenly, with pencil and paper, he looked up and said: "All these brothers have gone out to plant churches in different countries and are pastors and workers now." We could glorify God, because the multiplier effect of E.E. had been fulfilled.

Also, the "Cita con la Vida" Church, located in the city of Córdoba, adopted and used E.E. a lot for its growth. Pastor Carlos Belart was an intelligent worker, taking advantage of E.E. so that the church would do a clear evangelistic work permanently.

In Santa Fe, city of the homonymous province of Argentina, we trained again a local church in March 2011, the "Nueva Vida" Church, led by Pastor José Faienza and his wife. They were taking up the local ministry of E.E. after they had begun in 1991 and had planted 13 churches in the interior of the province. Now they were using E.E. again with new teaching models. We took Casati to teach. He was an old friend and well-known man of the local pastor and his wife. As she has a very fruitful ministry of counseling, she permanently used the presentation of the gospel for the task of counseling. He told us something surprising: He had a record of more than 3,000 faith decisions throughout those years. And added to this, that weekend of EV-2 (new E.E. material) training we had 176 faith decisions for the Glory of God!

Returning to the 80s, while this action continued in Argentina, the National Committee assumed the challenge of reaching Uruguay and Paraguay with the impetus given by the International Ministry for the Southern Cone region.

In the middle of that decade the work began in Uruguay. The Lord used pastor Alfredo Adjián, of the Armenian Evangelical Church of Montevideo.

Also, the pastor of the First Baptist Church, Lemuel Larrosa promised to develop E.E. clinics, which were carried out and implementations were developed. We visited with Daniel Perrone of the Armenian Church 20 years later and the believers remembered fondly those years, and even personally they used E.E. It was wonderful to find the fire burning there.

Clinics were taught in Paraguay during those years. Casati and Ernesto Humeniuk were trainers in the neighboring country. Pedro Berardo and Juan Manuel Monzón were pioneer developers in Paraguay, and were part of the first national committee. Also, a key man was pastor Alfredo Klassen. Of Mennonite background, passionate about making disciples and planting churches, for many years led the national ministry. He was very good in interpersonal relationships, saw that many workers of all denominations were trained in E.E. It is worth mentioning that he assumed the challenge of preaching in the most dangerous prison in Asunción, Paraguay, the prison of Tacumbú, and he did so for many years. The fruit among the interns was wonderful. Many desperate men found Jesus Christ and their lives were transformed. I remember that at a time when churches showed no interest in using E.E. in the last decade, Alfredo and his team continued visiting the prison to make disciples. He used to say, "If churches don't want it... the Lord wants the prisoners to be saved."

In each country, there was the right time and people that God chose to be useful tools at the national level. We mentioned some, but for each one of them, there were dozens that committedly carried out the sowing and harvest that the Lord had prepared for those years. Casati was always well received, admired and tremendously respected. His humility touched deeply everyone's hearts. He maintained ministry friendships for years and we must highlight the trust among them all. They were trustworthy people deeply focused on the Great

Commission. Everyone wanted Dr. Lajara to visit again their local churches, families and cities. The path that these two men established was leaving an immense mark of grace in the lives of all those with whom the Holy Spirit put in relationship. When we look at these processes in an integrated manner, we see the Providence of God working on his Redeeming Plan. Our God is Admirable!

Later period, years 1990 - 2009

The social, political and economic changes introduced in the 1990s in several countries of the region, affected the idea of projection that was considered in the first decade already described.

The advent of postmodernity, and the abrupt arrival in Latin America of post- Christianity brought new ways of thinking and developing churches.

Progressively the denominational constructions entered in different types of crisis, and that stopped the initial impulse of E.E. in the region. The emergence of neo-Pentecostalism and the new apostolic paradigm in Latin America generated a whole retraction in the mid-decade in the Southern Cone.

At the beginning of the 21st century, in a survey with pastors who had implemented E.E. in their churches 20 years before, they communicated to us a variety of causes for which they postponed or abandoned the use of the ministry, which they did not stop valuing, as they explained, but that people did not want long application processes, so they looked for other alternatives.

Obviously, the consumer culture overwhelmed Christians, and the life of the churches was affected by that deceptive way of seeing faith.

One of them was very sincere; an Argentine worker told us: "You saw how we Argentines are, we discontinue everything." In this way he explained to us the disinterest generated in people.

Many churches supported small-scale processes and many trainers continued preparing some new trainers and soul winners. The national committee had plans, but they were carried out with certain difficulties. But Lajara, Casati, Calcagni, Humeniuk, Perrone, Klassen, and so many others remained firm, with their hands on the plow, struggling with

111

clinics and its implementation as far as their efforts became possible.

As Casati was the Regional Director for the Southern Cone he continued encouraging leaders and processes in the region. He visited countries and supported its development in places where the doors were still open or opened. He always had local accompaniment and E.E. continued to bear fruit. He also permanently assisted Cecilio Lajara in everything related to material reviews and counseling countries outside the Southern Cone, in Latin America.

In March 1996, Casati along with John Calcagni, President of the Argentine Committee, were present at the Coral Ridge Presbyterian Church in Fort Lauderdale for E.E. World Congress events, as all the nations of the world had been reached, 211 in that moment, with the introduction and implementation of the E.E. ministry.

It was a glorious moment. All the directors and presidents of National Committees, together with the E.E. International Board, were in the services of Thanksgiving to God for having allowed to reach the world vision, all the countries working in one way or another with the national development of E.E. In three decades, the global expansion was achieved. Dr. D. James Kennedy, Senior Pastor of Coral Ridge, founder and President of E.E. worldwide, presided and preached in those services.

Now the challenges of a new period of time worldwide made E.E. think about its future, and its projection towards the 21st century. Several committees at the Board level engaged in praying, dreaming, thinking, suggesting and resolving towards that future. Then, as of 2003, an innovation process was presented worldwide and was progressively moved to regions across the globe. Dr. Lajara, as Vice President for Latin America, took the innovation processes to different countries under his responsibility.

There were different trainings, evaluations, investigations and decision making in the countries. Particularly, the initiative gained strength where E.E. was best organized and initiatives were taken to each region. Osvaldo Casati and Dr. Lajara were traveling to countries, visiting brothers, encouraging local and national processes.

In Argentina, a Baptist church that served as a clinic base in Lanús, Greater Buenos Aires, was strong. There pastor Alfonso Cubilla was still working and the church was bearing fruit with E.E. as the axis of this growth process. The church had begun in the pastor's house. His children, excellent coaches and disciples, took care of the people God gave them as new disciples of Jesus Christ. The National Committee planned several actions from that place. The Korean pastor and missionary Pedro Kang, who knew E.E. from his native Korea, also joined and wanted to multiply it in Argentina. The Mission "Santidad" Church, located in Buenos Aires, in the neighborhood of Boedo, began collaborating to multiply E.E. to all workers under its influence. And there, Daniel Perrone, local pastor and right hand of Pedro Kang, carried out the processes. Because Daniel belongs to the first generation of people trained by E.E., and has used it continuously for three decades, we want to share his testimony:

In the early years of the '80s, I met Evangelism Explosion in a clinic at the "Lanús de Cristo" Baptist Church, which Juan Calcagni was pastoring at the time. He directed the Woody Lajara Clinic.

It was really impressive to see the brothers of this church serving us with all joy, and going out to share the gospel personally. It was a week acquiring a lot of information, but also recognizing the loving purpose of God by offering such a beautiful and useful tool. It was a lot of time invested every day of that week at Woody's classes, but he made an impact, from his presence, his way of transmitting the teaching, as for his kindness and dedication. It was unforgettable. One of our outings was to the Lanús train station. There, with two friendly pastors, we had the opportunity to see how five people received the gift of eternal life.

In the middle of the week I already wanted to develop the plan as soon as possible in the church I was pastoring in Floresta. But we still had to complete the materials and take our exam.

I had been in the pastorate for several years, and with pastoral experience even before my ordination; but E.E. was a before and after for my way of evangelizing and preparing others to share the gospel. Because, before this I didn't have a strategy, or a tool, or material to prepare the believers to fulfill the Great Commission.

Thank God that after so many years the believers prepared at that time continued sharing the gospel and those received it remain firm and communicate the good news of the "gift of eternal life."

When we went with my family to Misiones, a province in northern Argentina, to serve the Lord there, we put the plan into practice. I cannot deny my gratitude to the

Lord for giving me the opportunity to share the gospel to so many people, and to see so many believers willing to be part of the planting. For some it was, as for myself, a before and after in his life.

When we returned to Buenos Aires, as always, we go with what we have and who we are. And E.E. has been a tremendous blessing. Thus, we began with three Missionary Works, and some of the believers who received the gospel and were discipled, are pastors today. And the fire of the Lord's presence is with them, over their lives, which leads them to keep sharing what they've received.

I participate in a Pastoral Training Center since about 15 years in Buenos Aires. We launched once a year, as part of the curriculum, "Share Your Faith". We have seen the hand of God working among us and the grace of God poured out in each church represented that has implemented the plan.

The first year we did the Clinic at the Training Center, pastors Osvaldo Casati and Guillermo Di Giovanna led and taught us, and later Will Rodríguez blessed us with his participation and teaching.

I must recognize with gratitude the life of those who over the years have served the Lord with disinterest and love, so that the church, both in Argentina and in Latin America, can take advantage of the blessing of Evangelism Explosion, Woody Lajara by planting, Juan Calcagni, pioneer in Argentina by implementing and teaching together with Osvaldo Casati and Ernesto Humeniuk. Their precious lives have been and are an example and challenge for my life and ministry.

They also gave me the opportunity to serve in E.E. as National Director. And I was able to actively participate for several years with their support, prayer, advice and accompaniment implementing it in Argentina, Uruguay, Chile and Paraguay about the renewed vision and materials of E.E. And in that way, I could also know precious men and women servants of the Lord who have given and give their lives for the growth and maturation of the church in their countries through E.E. I remember with love and respect Pastor Alfredo Klassen and his wife, Fermín González and his wife Antonia in Paraguay; Jovita Medel, Ruth Johana Figueroa Quesada and her husband Gabriel in Chile, Nelson Ibarra, Cristian González in Argentina and Will Rodríguez and Tatita, among other valuable and dear brothers.

I was able to participate in two Nations Congresses. There it was clearer the action of God in the world, just as it was so encouraging to meet lively brothers who serve the Lord every day extending His kingdom in their countries, many of them putting at risk their lives.

I must thank Pastor James Kennedy, who was faithful to the heavenly vision, and to those who went out into the world to share the E.E. vision, and for being able to do my small part in this, while I rejoice in the saving work of God.

In 2003, E.E. launched a search and development program for Field Workers worldwide. Through National Committees an agenda was established with the Vice President and the Regional Directors in order to look for possible candidates and share with them training times and have a selection of these new workers for the new stage of the worldwide ministry.

Osvaldo Casati worked on this goal for the Southern Cone. A date was established in September 2004 in Paraguay, and the selection was carried out, with the arrival of the Vice President, Dr. Cecilio Lajara, along with the brothers who came from Chile, Argentina, Paraguay, Colombia, etc. The survey process and subsequent innovation and the goals of establishing or renewing national committees were launched. The already reviewed 13-week materials, clinic manuals and all the field experience were going to accompany the new workers as useful tools.

The testing, translation and field tests of a new motivational tool, called "Share your Faith" began, with a workshop lasting a day and a half, to motivate, promote and teach the basics of the presentation of the gospel, with an outing of practical training as a demonstration.

Among Dr. Lajara's plans was a visit to Paraguay and Chile in 2005. We met in Paraguay for a motivational and promotional congress with brother Klassen and his wife, and E.E.-friendly churches and field workers. And then we arrived in Santiago, Chile, to work on testing the "Share your Faith" program with the believers of the First Presbyterian Church of Chile. It was a time to make contact with Brazilian Presbyterian missionaries serving at the Presbyterian Church of Chile, the friendly Chilean pastors and our team. Between memories and new challenges, we tested the tool there, and we motivated these churches to work with it. Joao Rocha acted as coordinator of these meetings in Chile. In Temuco, during the same week, we had a workshop with the Baptist and Alliance believers and some Pentecostals as well. The Coordinator, Joba Médel, did a fine job, lighting the fire of evangelization in many cities.

Pastor José Mardones, of the Alliance Church, opened its doors, and E.E. flourished again in that region. We began a new time and established the basis for a National Committee that could manage the processes. That week, in Santiago, Chile, the First Presbyterian Church provided its facilities. Woody Lajara, Osvaldo Casati, Pablo Méndez and the Regional Director for the Southern Cone candidate, Guillermo Di Giovanna of Argentina, also reviewed the material, translation and initial format of **"Share your faith."** Then, the name that we'd given it for the "brown" America arose: **"Manos a la Obra" [Share your faith]**, which has the impetus that we, the Latinos need, to move to action.

Pablo Méndez directed Colombia, but was also Director for South America. All the new workers, called Field Workers, who had joined in the region as of mid-2004, were under his mentoring. With a particular grace to lead and also to develop others, he was influencing the task of each one, guiding the different personal challenges and the task to be done. His wife Argelia accompanied him, to work with the sisters, and we were able to meet and be blessed by God through this family committed to the Lord's work. His ability to relate in a friendly way and to help others, his integrity and gentleness, was a resource used by God to strengthen and develop all new workers.

In those years the Fifth Presbyterian Church of Santiago became a clinic base; the Sixth Church in Las Condes, presided by pastor Leandro de Almeida Pinheiro, also opened its doors. We had E.E. Adult clinics in Santiago and Temuco, where the process grew at the Second Baptist Church, of Santa Rosa neighborhood. There pastor Angel Montenegro collaborated and had joined the National Committee in 2005. There were "Share Your Faith" workshops in all those churches and many more that Jovita Médel reported, also the training for Teachers of Clinics. Later, in 2007 we introduced E.E. Youth. Guillermo Salinas visited us, a Presbyterian missionary in Mexico, a church planter who led the development of E.E. Youth on the continent. In Chile, the Coordinator Jovita Médel did a tenacious work, lighting the fire of evangelization in many churches of different cities. Then Joao Petrecelli, another Brazilian missionary who arrived in Santiago, Chile, continued training trainers at the Fifth Presbyterian Church. In that period José Mardones was president of the National Committee, the man who had the dream in 1982 of bringing E.E. to Chile, was still promoting the vision.

These steps were taken in Argentina simultaneously. Workshops, clinics and the process of building a national ministry strongly demanded all the effort of its participants. The experience of Casati and Calcagni inspired confidence to be permanently advised on how to move forward.

At the end of 2004 it was necessary to expand and develop a team for Argentina, which was the driving country of the region. We began to pray and act. There was an action unit with Juan Calcagni, Osvaldo Casati, Alberto Aisncough and Rosa, Daniel Perrone and Lidia, Pedro Kang and Alfonso Cubilla. They all offered and progressively accompanied with their churches, acted and participated directly in the growth of the work in Argentina and the Southern Cone, since, for example, Alfonso helped us in Paraguay and later Daniel would do it in Chile for a while.

Dr. Lajara's visits and mentoring were now possible thanks to the use of new communications online, including emails and Skype, allowed a close dialogue and better monitoring. It also digitized all feedback in electronic forms, facilitating the flow of information on what was happening on the continent.

The Latin American Team meetings, in which we participated with Casati, were extremely enriching. We traveled to Villeta, Colombia, where we continued to receive instructions, and interacted with all the workers in Latin America. Pablo Méndez and Algeria had organized and made the logistics of the meeting in order to receive all Latin America workers that could arrive. They did a formidable task. In April 2007, Ron Tyler granted to Casati an honorary plaque for 25 years of service. After accompanying Casati for two and a half years, I took responsibility of the Southern Cone. We continued traveling together, teaching, and particularly his mentoring was extraordinary to do a task that exceeded all our own human possibilities.

We needed to seek pastors interested in training and implementing in local churches. Efforts were many: To produce printing materials or photocopying of good quality, traveling to train, to motivate and encourage. Organizing national teams so that the processes have continuity and efficiency. Raising support and maintenance funds for field workers in the operational area. The prayer support of the Korean brothers in Latin America and the USA was really significant. The churches that held us in prayer also in Korea made us see the active power of the Holy Spirit, guiding, correcting, mobilizing, involving people and especially bringing salvation in many places. At one point, Pedro Kang sent prayer bulletins by email to 1700 intercession contacts in Korea every month. And the prayer vigils, carried out in the local church of the neighborhood of Boedo, had immense response in the tasks of the countries of the Southern Cone region. And the same thing happened everywhere, the premise was to assess whether things were going well, or if things didn't work out it was due to the weakness in prayer life, which should accompany the life of each disciple. And where prayer flourished, which is the search and dependence of the Lord, then the ministry flourished. This leads us to recognize that it was God's strength, not ours. It was the wisdom of God, His pure grace and mercy that did the work in the Southern Cone and throughout the continent. It was what Dr. D. James Kennedy had taught us, always emphasizing the words of the prophet Jeremiah in chapter 33:3, "Call to me, and I will answer you, and teach you great and unsearchable things that you do not know."

In 2006 we moved to Bahía Blanca with María Alejandra, my wife. As Regional Director of the Southern Cone, I had the responsibility to attend the countries of the area. I could get by bus to Temuco in a day, then go to the central south of Chile and accompany Jovita Médel, who lived in the area. We gathered the Committee there and stayed for the national ministry under construction. It was the place where we recruited the marriage of Gabriel Tatin and Ruth Figueroa, who were progressively growing in the ministry.

In that year, we began introducing E.E. at the "Pueblo Nuevo" Baptist Church in Bahía Blanca. Pastor Néstor Golluscio reopened the local doors for training and implementation. We made the first materials, and praying to the Lord, He guided us to train one of their pastors, who then took care of the youth area, brother Carlos Ibarra. He accepted the challenge in a very good attitude, and undertook the path of training in E.E. We had adult and youth clinics, with the visit of Guillermo Salinas from Mexico. And we were developing a local team, within the three-year vision, which today supports the national ministry of E.E. Argentina. Carlos accompanied me to Chile, because he had a feeling of closeness for the neighboring country, as his father was of Chilean origin. And there, in Santiago he graduated in the E.E. Adult clinic, and in other training. He adopted the vision and the local church continued growing. In 2007, it broke a stagnant situation and the sustained growth started again, passing the thousand-member barrier. Carlos joined the national team and became the president. After many years, he took Juan Calcagni's place. We verified again, in the 21st century, that the three-year vision was still as applicable and fruitful, as the brothers of the previous generation taught us. Meanwhile, in Buenos Aires, Daniel Perrone continued in charge and Casati continued helping him. And pastor Alfonso Cubilla, was still working in the southern part of Greater Buenos Aires.

In Paraguay, Alfredo Klassen encouraged the same processes, while the thirteen-week trainings continued; we took "Share Your Faith" and E.E. Youth. A disciple of Alfredo, pastor Fermín González Ocampo, joined the task with his wife. Then we could see how the work flourished towards younger generations. We traveled with Daniel Perrone several times to encourage these tools and saw an opening to develop them.

In Uruguay, the Armenian Evangelical Church opened its doors to us once again. We had a workshop with 70 young people and then they multiplied it in summer campaigns in the interior of the country, where they preached in different towns and cities. The main pastor, Pedro Lapadjián, is a leader in evangelization in the country and pastor Ricardo Aprikián, youth pastor, carried out the local process, within the objectives of that church.

In 2008 the Latin American Team met again for the management of the continental task in Bogotá, Colombia. We continued to accompany national and regional processes, and we joined more and more in the objectives of the continental ministry. Casati still accompanied us in that meeting at the Convent of Usaquén. The continental ministry was preparing for the next steps, which had the task of organizing an E.E. World Congress and a new way of guiding the ministry globally. We were accompanied by Dr. Ron Tyler, E.E. Global Vice President, who had been recruited by Dr. Lajara for his service in this ministry many years ago. At that meeting, we proposed Dr. Ernesto Humeniuk, who lived in Miami, as a member of the Board, representing Latin America. He was replacing sister Rosita de Ainscough, who had been in that role before. Ernesto accepted the challenge and his nomination was accepted in E.E.

While a new stage was being promoted in the countries, the E.E. Continental Team of Directors helped to solve local problems, guided the search for willing leaders, local churches and new challenges on the horizon to undertake. An important desire was to bring the model that E.E. already had for Kids' Evangelism, which worked in Latin America, but we hadn't been able to develop it in the Southern Cone. For that reason, three sisters came to train to Bogotá. An important clinic of E.E. Kids was developed at "El Camino" Baptist Church, under the responsibility of Algeria Morales de Méndez. The sisters Tania Mattiussi of Petreceli, Miriam Lago Moncada de Vilchez, who served in Chile, would return to prepare other sisters in the Fifth Presbyterian Church of Santiago. And, Lidia Vartani de Perrone, from Argentina, would do the same in that country. We wanted to achieve this goal and take it to Paraguay and Uruguay. Sister Lidia Vartani de Perrone shares her experience with E.E. as she has been linked with her husband for about three decades and took on the challenge of being responsible of this ministry focused on kids for Argentina:

With this testimony I want to praise the Lord for the Ministry of Evangelism Explosion, especially for Hope for Kids.

In 2008, I received the invitation of Pastor Guillermo Di Giovanna, to participate in the Kids Hope Clinic for Latin American countries, in Bogotá, Colombia.

I saw God's confirmation in His provision for the trip, and as a teacher, when I asked my Supervisor for permission, she told me to take the days I needed since this was going to be for the good of the kids in Argentina.

So, I was able to participate there with joy, because God renewed his call: "... See, I have placed before you an open door. I know that you have little strength, yet you have kept my word and have not denied my name." Rev.3.8

Since my adolescence I consecrated my life to the Lord and knew that this "door" was kids, for that reason I prepared myself as a teacher in the Word, and I was able to share the gospel with them.

In this clinic I was impressed by the simplicity of the lessons to communicate the gospel to the children, and the love with which the church had prepared everything, Mr. and Mrs. Méndez, and Cristina Blanquel.

Undoubtedly, what marked that experience the most was the outing we made to a Day Home for street children. There I presented the gospel to girls of 12 and 13 years of age. They told me their experiences, knew all the evils of the street and felt unworthy. When they understood that God loved them and gave his Son, they received him in their hearts and wept with repentance and joy. I could see how simple it was to share the gospel and the fruit it gave.

So I returned with enthusiasm and made a call to the church because I needed collaborators to work as a team. With four young people we began to prepare the materials and we moved on to do the task. Several teachers were trained.

Many neighborhood children met Jesus as their Savior; some, already teenagers, are still faithful, others are in another country and church. A girl died in an accident, but hours earlier she expressed her security of the gift of eternal life. Others, we don't know, but they heard of God's love.

We also prepared several clinics with the church, where a good group of teachers was trained. We were able to collaborate in clinics of other churches.

I thank the Lord for everything, without doubts Hope for Kids is a beautiful tool for children to know the Lord!

Some things had happened in 2008, between winter and spring, which indicated the urgency of starting the work with kids.

The first thing was that, at the Youth Clinic in Santiago, pastor Leandro de Almeyda Pinheiro urged us to bring the kids program to Chile. The second thing was that, upon returning home, about a month later, there was a call with a very delicate request from sister María Laura Vázquez. She worked as a pediatric nurse in intensive therapy at the Regional Hospital "José Penna" in the city of Bahía Blanca. She asked me to visit the therapy area where a 10-year-old boy was in the terminal phase, and asked to see a pastor. I immediately left my work and I went to that place. They explained to me that the child was from a nearby city, and that there was no chance of life, due to his condition. But since he went to an evangelical church in his city, he wanted to see a pastor. What a strong experience! When I approached the bed, I took his hand and called him by his name, and began to pray. When I began praying, he just went into a crisis and died. I called the medical staff, they approached, having nothing more to do. Then I talked to the mother, who was obviously crying. Later, I returned home, and while driving I understood something very simple, but deeply related to the Lord's redemptive purposes: that child was a believer. He had gone to heaven to be with the Lord. And what about so many others who didn't know the gift of eternal life? Without doubt, it was a priority to bring E.E. Kids to the Southern Cone.

Among so many chores and so many demands, we were always setting the priorities in prayer and setting the goals of each year, in order to achieve those objectives. And with so much work, this had been postponed in the Southern Cone, but now was the right time.

Then, in 2009, we were invited to attend a meeting of Regional Directors and other world leaders in Fiji, Oceania. This meeting took place in August and early September, 2009. We had a very good experience at cross-cultural level, with the members of E.E. We met the Vice Presidents of the continents, and many of their collaborators. The meeting was led by Dr. John Sorensen, World President of the ministry. We personally witnessed there the program of transition towards the E.E. World Congress, which would take place in Kuala Lumpur, Malaysia in March 2010. And it was there in Fiji that we had the first Theological Education experience in a program that was being implemented for the staff and would be launched to the continents; created by Dr. Cecilio Lajara, called "Advanced Studies in the Great Commission." We also had Dr. Paul R. Gilchrist, as a teacher and facilitator. The courses "He Gave us Prophets" and "Kingdom, Covenants and Canon" from the Third Millennium Ministries curriculum were taught; in agreement with E.E., he gave us the courses to train the workers. It was an extraordinary time with Fiji pastors, who joined the classes. Friendship is very important in the islands of Oceania, and they offered us their meals, music, joy and friendship.

We lived in Fiji many memorable moments. One of them was to share a devotional for everyone present, with the help of other members of the Latin American team. Robert Foster helped with English readings, in order to read with good pronunciation, and at the end of the devotional, Dr. John Sorensen and Dr. Ron Tyler gave an honorary plaque to Dr. Lajara for his years of service in E.E. with many major responsibilities, including Senior Vice President at one time and Vice President of Latin America and the Iberian Peninsula for many years.

Dr. Lajara had introduced E.E. in more than 80 countries, making travel arrangements, and starting contact work in order to have future clinics, choosing leaders that would encourage national work, etc. At that time, he was leaving the role as Vice President for Latin America in the hands of Wilfredo Rodríguez, a Puerto Rican disciple. And Dr. Cecilio Nicolás Lajara was in charge of the project for Advanced Studies in the Great Commission, which was designed by request of the E.E. Board with the support of John Knox Seminary, of the Coral Ridge Presbyterian Church in Fort Lauderdale.

We were in preparation for a project called Hope for Kids, in global management, and we received the first instructions in Fiji. E.E. already had a training model focused on kids, which worked on our continent, but we hadn't been able to develop it in the Southern Cone. However, as we mentioned before, we had already trained three sisters who made the first materials. This new project gave a new impetus to E.E. Kids, it had a new design and it was easier to implement. This project also counted with donations for the printing material to train many churches and a lot of training donations for its implementation.

So, we were facing answered prayer, so that we could multiply the model of children's evangelism with many churches. God is kind! And at the same time, we had prepared ground, sister leaders who had already prepared collaborators in Chile and Argentina, which would facilitate the implementation and multiplication of that project.

2010 – 2012 Period

We went to Costa Rica in January 2010, and there we saw more details of everything that would come to Latin America. Ron Tyler, the E.E. Global Vice President, instructed the leaders of the multipliers countries to go to Kuala Lumpur to sign the "Covenant of Nations" at the Congress of the Nations, for a period of multiplication and development of mature nations, where they were going to encourage growing nations and emerging countries to grow. March 2010 was coming and we would meet in Kuala Lumpur, Malaysia. Meanwhile, we were now under the direction of Wilfredo Rodríguez, collaborating with his management to strengthen his continental leadership.

Dr. Lajara was also there to teach along with Paul R. Gilchrist, in the first Spanish course of the Advanced Studies in the Great Commission program. It was a wonderful week of theological studies, fellowship, guidance and inspiration for the continental ministry.

There, a tribute to Dr. Lajara and his wife Carmen was paid, who arrived for a service of Thanksgiving to God. It took place on Thursday, January 10, in San José, Costa Rica. And Rev. Juan R. Rivera Medina from Puerto Rico, Woody's old friend, preached based on Philippians 2:29-30. In that service his work of more than 29 years was recognized serving in E.E.

First Congress of the Nations in Kuala Lumpur

We arrived at the Congress of Nations. There was signed the Covenant of Nations which started a process of growth from commands established in sessions with the E.E. Board during the Congress, which should lead to its implementation, through Vice Presidents, in cooperation with the countries identified as "mature." Each signatory country had the conditions of operation, government, and sustainability, in order to be in charge of another growing country and progressively lead it to an M country, that is, "mature."

Those days all the delegates met to discuss various topics, which would be approved by the Congress of Nations, including the E.E. Indigenization Document, pointing the way of inculturation ministry in different countries and regions. It was my turn, on the direction of Ron Tyler, to sign the covenant, on behalf of Argentina, as a "mature" or multiplier country. The National Committee supported that decision. We would then have the duty to accompany Chile, as a growing country for several years, until 2016, when they assumed their new status as a mature country, at the Indonesian World Congress. And in the case of Paraguay, it would be an emerging country, which we should also develop.

Upon my return from this event, which began a new stage, and with new challenges and a new way of global operation for E.E. we had to launch Hope for Kids.

We started to plan the activities with the sisters from Chile and Argentina, and Cristina Blanquel de Vega, the sister in charge of the continental ministry would visit us from Mexico. In October, from 9 to 11, we had the Hope for Kids workshop at "Vida Nueva" Church, in Buenos Aires. That ministry is also known as H4K, (Hope for Kids). We trained 28 churches, and 20 were added to E.E. Pastor Daniel Perrone and his wife Lidia were hosts, and we began a process of multiplication in that ministry with the opening of "LAPEN" (APEN) that allowed us to call their instructors to train many churches after this initial event. Sisters from Paraguay and Uruguay were trained, so that we could take this ministry to these countries as well.

In that same month, a few days later, October 15-17, we had the same training in Santiago, Chile, for 25 churches, which began the multiplication of Hope for Kids.

We were in a precious and strategic time of multiplication. God had answered prayers, and now we were planning 2011 and 2012 with these workshops to train kids, and new tools like EV2, which we were beginning to develop in the region.

In fact, in 2010 we had 16 workshops of "Share Your Faith" in the region. 264 people were trained, including 12 pastors, and 15 churches added this E.E. tool.

We had these two "Hope for Kids" workshops (already mentioned), one E.E. Clinic for Adults and a launch of Effective Evangelism. In the latter, 86 people were trained in Ev2. The interesting thing was that the gospel was presented to 303 people, with 133 decisions of faith and 39 of security of salvation. We had now 41 new churches and we train 19 pastors.

A team was formed in Chile, with a new worker, Ruth Figueroa Quezada and a National Director, brother Ángel Montenegro, as well as other volunteer workers. Two new workers joined in Argentina, one of them, brother Cristian Gonzalez, who was later the National Director. Wilfredo Rodríguez came to the Southern Cone to establish the new workers; we had meetings in Buenos Aires and Santiago de Chile.

Many local churches continued their 13-week training of the Classic E.E and Youth E.E.

And in August 2010, Dr. Cecilio Lajara and his wife Carmen arrived in Buenos Aires, to teach an Advanced Studies course on the Great Commission.

It was a very intense year, with many trips and a lot of work. But very blessed by God.

125

At the temple of the "Santidad" Church, in Buenos Aires, where we had a base, an Old Testament course was taught by Dr. Daniel Santos, from the Andrew Jumper School of Theology at McKenzie University in Sao Paulo, Brazil.

It was a time of edification, together with a group of pastors from the "Centro de Capacitación Pastoral Bernabé" [Barnabas Pastoral Training Center] which depended on pastor Pedro Kang and Daniel Perrone as mentors.

As we have reviewed, this year in the global plan was a stage for new developments of E.E. in different countries. So, after a year of intense work, we had to be able to consolidate the initiated processes and sustain the development of local multiplication processes.

The challenge was immense in itself, and a series of approaches were given by people who assumed support roles to sustain the work.

Without a doubt, we were increasingly understanding how to do tasks and work in teams. And in each country, more kids' workshops and the implementation that should accompany these trainings were being developed.

They were years of intense work, and with the digital reporting system, it was possible to provide real-time information about what was happening.

The year 2011 went by, and in September 2012 we attended a meeting of National and Regional Directors in Fiji, with the E.E. world authorities. It was on that trip that we found Daniel Perrone, National Director of Argentina, working on the development of the region and accompanying the growth of Chile step by step. And they encouraged us to develop implementation with balanced and intelligent efforts to all the workers.

We were also told all about the Second World Congress, to be held in South Africa in 2013. Daniel Perrone and Carlos Ibarra would travel there, Carlos as President of E.E. in Argentina. And there, in Fiji, we were informed that, as of 2013, the position of Regional Directors would no longer exist, since the development was now in the hands of mature countries, which through their National Directors and in agreement with the growing countries, should establish action plans and carry them forward; therefore, the task of Regional Directors was no longer needed in the new E.E. design.

That was how I presented my resignation in January 2013, after having provided all relevant information to the Vice President, Wilfredo Rodríguez (picture at the right) and the National Committee of E.E. Argentina. I remained collaborating with the National Committee as an Advisor and with the Committee of Chile, mentoring the Field Workers until the end of 2014.

My conviction is that the Lord had called me in 2004 through Casati, Lajara and Pablo Méndez for this stage of revitalization of E.E. in the Southern Cone. And that was accomplished by the grace of God. That task required all the support they gave me, and gave to the countries. All their effort made possible to expand the action of national ministries. In addition, being part of the Team of Continental Directors, that Dr. Lajara had created, was very honorable for me and allowed me to learn and grow together with those responsible of the continent.

When plans of the First World Congress arrived, there was prepared ground for the expansion that E.E. had designed. By consolidating this process, and removing the role to which I had been called, for which I had been lovingly trained by them, I did not find, in my opinion, a position for me in the organizational chart. All my mentors had retired from continental leadership as well. And I understood that I had to cease my functions by order of the World Congress, and because the time for that service came to an end. I can sincerely remember the words of Jesus: *"So you also, when you have done everything you were told to do, should say: We are unworthy SERVANTS, we have only done our duty."* Luke 17:10.

I thank God for all these years of service and the relations generated, which made possible to live an intense experience in the evangelization of the continent. For each church that opened its doors in different countries, for every teaching opportunity, to testify and motivate others making disciples, to write these pages with former colleagues and brothers, has been to revive the powerful grace of God in His people on the continent. Praise our Great God and Savior!

Leaders of Evangelism Explosion of Ibero-America in Costa Rica, 2010.

Biographical data of Dr. Cecilio N. Lajara

Dr. Cecilio (Woody) Lajara was born in Puerto Rico and has served the Lord since his youth. His mother, Camelia Lajara Rodriguez, made sure that her son received Christian education since childhood. He grew up in the Presbyterian Church of Puerto Rico and after finishing his college career at the University of Puerto Rico, he studied theology at the Presbyterian "Columbia Theological Seminary," in Decatur, Georgia, where he received a Degree in Master of Divinity and Master of Theology. He received his doctoral degrees at Emory University and Luther Rice College & Seminary, both in Atlanta, Georgia.

Being from our "Brown" America, as he usually calls the Latin American continent, Dr. Lajara has served in various ministerial capacities. After serving as the founding pastor of the First Spanish Presbyterian Church in Atlanta, he went to the Mission Field for several years. In Mexico he was Professor of Systematic Theology at the Presbyterian Theological Seminary. In Guatemala he was the founder and organizer of the School of Theology of the Mariano Gálvez University. He participated in the organization of the Logoi Pastoral Program and was the creator and organizer of the Latin American Faculty of Theological Studies (FLET), which he developed as his doctoral thesis. Dr. Lajara, together with Dr. Paul Gilchrist and Dr. Rick Perrin, were the creators and developers of the World Reformed Fellowship (WRF).

Dr. Lajara is currently retired after having worked for more than 40 years as a missionary with the Mission Board of the Presbyterian Church of America (PCA), and the Ministry of Evangelism Explosion, where he served as International Director (1994-96) and as Vice President for the Latin America continent.

He was one of the founders of several international organizations, including the Confraternidad Latinoamericano de Iglesia Reformadas (C.L.I.R) [Confraternity of L.A. Reformed Churches]. Currently, after his retirement and with some leaders, he has organized the online Knox Theological Seminary, which has been developed for Latin America and Spain.

Dr. Lajara is married to Carmen Sánchez Lugo. With expressions of gratitude to God, they have completed 55 years of marriage. They have three children (Iris, Mariselle and Juan; and three grandchildren (Melina 22, Caleb 20 and Victoria 16).

www.ingramcontent.com/pod-product-compliance
Lightning Source LLC
Chambersburg PA
CBHW061145040426
42445CB00013B/1567